My Best To You

Best wishes,
Bonnie Paiva

A Collection of
Choice Recipes
for the New Cook

BONNIE S. PAIVA

Copyright © 1992 by Bonnie S. Paiva

Copies of

My Best To You

May be obtained from:

My Best To You
P.O. Box 3041
Farmington Hills, MI 48333

ISBN 0-9639227-1-8

Copyright © 1992
Bonnie S. Paiva

All Rights Reserved

Cover Design by
The Word Baron, Inc.
Farmington Hills, MI

Published by
Document Design
West Bloomfield, MI

ACKNOWLEDGMENTS

Without the help I received from my daughter, Karen Carlson, this book would not have been possible. She bullied me into buying a computer, taught me to use it to an extent and what I could not do with the "machine" she did for me. She also edited, complimented, criticized and did all the things necessary to spur me on. Thanks, love!

Also, my thanks to all the cooks, chefs and others who develop recipes and publish them so that I can add them to my collection and publish them in this format. Collecting recipes has been my hobby for years and I think these are the best of the lot.

PREFACE

When I was married almost 40 years ago, I could not cook at all!! To my consternation I found that the man I married not only liked to eat, he liked all kinds of foods. Having been born and raised in Hawaii, he had been exposed to foods from all corners of the earth - and liked them all.

Hence, my interest in collecting and trying all kinds of recipes. My husband and later my children, were always willing to try any new dish I put before them. They were also very vocal in telling me what they liked and what they did not like. When the reception to any dish was bad, the recipe was thrown away. Notes and changes were made on others.

In 1981 we were expecting fourteen wedding invitations. In a state of panic about the costs of nice gifts for fourteen couples, I had to come up with an idea to keep the cost down and keep my family off bread and water. I found a unique, handcrafted wooden recipe box that was oversized and very

Preface

attractive. The little man in North Carolina who made these and the store personnel are still wondering why I needed fourteen recipe boxes.

To make these gifts original, I selected about 50 of my favorite recipes and typed them on cards and then added comments and instructions that I thought would be helpful to the new cook.

The reception was astounding. Not only did I get a glowing "thank you" from each couple, but I received notes from mothers and mothers-in-law. They were the best received gifts I've ever given.

The suggestion to write this book came from those couples, their parents, my children, my husband and my friends.

DEDICATION

This book is for new cooks because I think they need and deserve a collection of recipes to get them through day-to-day cooking, as well as recipes that will let them entertain their family, friends or even the boss with ease.

It is not meant to replace a good basic cookbook that gives you all kinds of information on nutrition, equivalents and substitutions, as well as tips on entertaining, how to store foods, plus hundreds of recipes. You will use the basic cookbook constantly as a reference book, if nothing else.

As you start your collection of recipes, be very selective about the cookbooks you buy. They are expensive and some are totally useless. I have a number of the useless variety (and I would list them for you but I'd probably be in for some legal action).

Some of the very best recipes are found in the food section of newspapers and magazines, especially

Dedication

gourmet magazines, and on food containers. And your friends and relatives will usually be very flattered if you ask for a recipe from them.

I would suggest that any time you try a recipe for the first time that you follow the directions very closely. Then you can change and take notes and make the recipe your very own.

TABLE OF CONTENTS

ON FOLLOWING DIRECTIONS iii

SOME THINGS YOU SHOULD KNOW v

APPETIZERS AND SNACKS 1

SALADS AND SALAD DRESSINGS 31

SOUPS AND STEWS 65

BEEF AND VEAL 87

PORK 123

POULTRY 145

SEAFOOD 171

SIDE DISHES 197

BREADS, MUFFINS AND SUCH 225

DESSERTS 243

COOKIES AND BARS 271

BREAKFAST OR BRUNCH 287

BEVERAGES 295

ON FOLLOWING DIRECTIONS

Some of these recipes are so simple that you may wonder why I even bothered to put them on paper. Others are a little more complicated, but none are beyond the ability of the most inexperienced cook. Just because a recipe calls for a long list of ingredients or the directions are long does not mean it is complicated.

Most recipes in most cookbooks have very clear instructions. However, some I do not understand at all. This is the reason you should always read a recipe through before attempting it. I once found a recipe for Stuffed Baked Lobster that sounded heavenly, but upon reading further I found that the instructions read "Prepare the live lobster for cooking by splitting down the center of the underside." Now, would you do that to a live lobster? Not I!!

I have attempted to make my instructions as clear as possible. However, no two cooks are going to interpret the directions the exact same way. A slight difference will not matter. Who knows? It might be better your way!

When baking, always follow the directions as closely as possible. Too much or too little of any number of ingredients can cause an instant failure.

You will find that I have used brand names in quite a few recipes. You do not necessarily need to use these brands but you will at least know what to look for.

GOOD LUCK AND GOOD EATING !

SOME THINGS YOU SHOULD KNOW

For some of you who have been well taught by your mothers to cook, this will all sound elementary. But for the real beginner these suggestions will be helpful. If you've read the previous pages, you will find that I am repeating some information. That is because not everyone is going to read dry, old introductions and such. In comments on the different recipes, I've repeated myself again for those who go directly to the recipes (overlooking all my fine advice and instructions at the beginning). Anyway, I had to fill up these pages with something!

* First and foremost, always read the recipe completely through before starting. It is very disconcerting to start a dish and find, when you are half way through, that you need something you do not have or a technique is called for that you are not familiar with.

* Lengthy recipes are not necessarily hard to make. Don't be intimidated. Read them through. Some are very simple.

* When a choice of ingredients is given, the first one mentioned is the one preferred. For instance, butter or margarine. Butter is expensive, true, but is so much better. The unsalted (sweet) butter is best for cooking.

* Try to plan menus for a week at a time. Make a complete list before shopping and stick to it. Not only will you save money, but you won't be without some ingredient you need for recipes that you've chosen for that week.

* It is said that only the very rich can afford to buy cheap. They can afford to toss out foods or other things that are not as they should be. Choose your grocery store, fruit market and butcher shop carefully. In some cases, you may pay a little more than the store down the street is charging, but nothing is more costly than a head of lettuce that is brown on the inside or a bag of oranges that are dry and tasteless.

Some Things You Should Know

- Cents-off coupons are only a savings method if you like and use that product or if you really want to try it. I have a friend who says she saves a fortune by using coupons, but her pantry is overflowing with products she doesn't use.
- When buying pots and pans and knives, buy the very best you can possibly afford. Not only will they make a great difference in your cooking, but they will last so much longer.
- A garlic press is an inexpensive item and will be used constantly (especially with my recipes!).
- The plastic vegetable spinner is the greatest invention since sliced bread. It spins the water from freshly washed salad greens in a jiffy.
- To store lettuce or any other greens, such as spinach, first clean well and dry in the vegetable spinner or on paper towels. Put 2 or 3 paper towels in the bottom of a plastic bag. Put the greens in the bag and refrigerate. Lettuce and greens will become nice and crisp and will keep for several days.
- When making salads, never cut the lettuce. Always tear it up into bite size pieces. Cut lettuce will turn brown in a very short time, but even if it is used immediately, it is harder to coat well with salad dressing.
- To peel tomatoes, put them in boiling water for about 40 to 60 seconds. When removed, the skin will peel off very easily. This works with peaches also.
- When a recipe calls for raw egg yolks to be put into a hot mixture, always put a little of the hot mixture into the egg yolks first, stir and then add the egg yolks to the hot mixture. This warms the egg yolks slightly and prevents curdling.

Some Things You Should Know

* A freezer can be a cook's best friend, especially for one who works outside the home. It can save you lots of time and money. Buy cuts of meat when they are on sale and freeze them. Cook large amounts of your favorite dishes and freeze them for a later date. Bake and freeze cookies. Keep some appetizers in the freezer for unexpected guests. You'll find a multitude of uses for your freezer.

* When freezing soups or other liquids, be sure to leave at least a 1-inch "headroom". The liquid will expand when frozen.

* Potatoes and pasta (spaghetti, macaroni, etc.) do not freeze well at all. If you want to freeze a dish that contains potatoes or pasta, freeze the dish, but wait to add the potatoes or pasta until you are ready to serve it. There are some exceptions. For instance, lasagna freezes very well.

* Please, please do not use "instant" rice in any recipe, especially mine. It does not taste like rice, does not cook up like rice and can ruin any dish in which you use rice.

APPETIZERS AND SNACKS

Most of these recipes are not found in any basic cookbook or any other book for that matter. Therefore, there are no cheese balls, finger sandwiches and other types of common appetizers, because they can be found almost anywhere. These recipes, I hope, are a little unique.

❦ COTTAGE AND BLUE CHEESE DIP ❦

Makes 1½ cups.

- 1 cup small curd cottage cheese
- ¼ pound blue cheese, crumbled
- 1 medium onion, thinly sliced
- ¼ cup sour cream
- Dash each of Worcestershire sauce and Tabasco sauce
- Small sliver of garlic

Place all ingredients in blender container and process until smooth. Serve with crackers, chips or crudites.

❦ HERB DIP WITH DILL AND CHIVES ❦

Makes about 2 cups.

- 1 cup small curd cottage cheese
- ½ cup mayonnaise
- ¼ cup sour cream
- 1 garlic clove, minced
- 2 tablespoons fresh dill, chopped or 2 teaspoons dried dill weed
- 1 teaspoon Worcestershire sauce
- 1 tablespoon chopped fresh chives or 1 teaspoon dried chives
- ½ teaspoon salt
- Dash of Tabasco sauce

Combine all ingredients, except crudites, in a medium bowl and mix well. Cover and refrigerate overnight. Serve with crudites, such as carrot sticks, celery sticks, cauliflower flowerets and such.

🍄 BACON DIP 🍄

Good with crackers, chips or vegetables.

Makes about 2 cups.

- 1 8-ounce package cream cheese, softened
- 4 slices cooked bacon, crisp and crumbled
- 1/2 cup sour cream
- 2 tablespoons snipped fresh chives*
- Salt and pepper to taste

Beat cream cheese in small bowl until fluffy. Blend in remaining ingredients.

*Dried chives can be used, but fresh chives are better. If you use dried chives, use only 1 teaspoon.

🍄 CLAMDIGGERS DIP 🍄

Makes 1 1/4 cups.

- 1 7 1/2-ounce can minced clams
- 1 8-ounce package cream cheese, softened
- 1 tablespoon lemon juice
- 1 teaspoon Worcestershire sauce
- 1 tablespoon grated onion
- 1 teaspoon chopped parsley
- 1/4 teaspoon salt
- 1/8 teaspoon Tabasco sauce
- Chips or crackers

Drain clams and reserve liquid. Combine cream cheese and lemon juice. Add seasonings and clams. Mix thoroughly. Chill for at least 1 hour to blend flavors. If it necessary to thin the dip, add the clam juice gradually.

❦ SCALLION AND BLUE CHEESE DIP ❦

Makes about 1½ cups.

- ¼ pound blue cheese, crumbled
- ½ cup sour cream
- ½ cup mayonnaise
- 6 scallions, sliced
- 1 garlic clove, chopped
- 2 tablespoons white-wine vinegar
- 2 tablespoons olive oil
- 1 tablespoon fresh lemon juice
- ½ teaspoon salt or to taste
- Cayenne pepper to taste

In a food processor or blender puree all ingredients until smooth.

Serve with crudites, such as carrot sticks, celery sticks, zucchini sticks or other raw vegetables.

❦ CRABMEAT DIP ❦

Makes 2½ cups.

- ¾ cup mayonnaise
- 1 6-ounce can crabmeat, drained and rinsed
- ⅓ cup finely chopped green pepper
- ⅓ cup canned tomato, drained, seeded, chopped
- 1 teaspoon chopped green onion (white part only)
- Ground pepper (black or red)

Combine all ingredients and mix well. Cover and chill.

Serve with crackers or chips.

🌱 BRAUNSCHWEIGER DIP 🌱

Makes about 1 cup.

    4 ounces braunschweiger
    1/2 cup sour cream
    2 tablespoons chopped green onion
    Salt and pepper to taste
    Assorted crackers

Combine braunschweiger and sour cream in medium bowl. Stir in onion, salt and pepper. Cover and refrigerate. Serve with crackers.

🌱 BARBECUED COCKTAIL SAUSAGES 🌱

The quickest and one of the best appetizers I've ever found.

    1 1-pound package of Hormel Cocktail Smokies
    Barbecue sauce (I use Hunt's Thick and Rich)

Put the sausages in a saucepan and cover with barbecue sauce. Heat through. Serve with assorted crackers and provide toothpicks. You can't get any simpler than that.

❦ SPICY CREAM CHEESE DIP ❦

Makes 1 cup.

    1 8 ounce package cream cheese
  1/4 cup picante sauce
       Juice of 1 lemon
       Salt and pepper to taste

Soften cream cheese. Combine all ingredients, blending well. Serve with corn chips, tortilla chips, potato chips or crackers.

❦ GUACAMOLE ❦

Makes about 2 cups.

  2 tablespoons finely minced onion
  1 to 2 chili peppers, seeded and coarsely chopped
  1 teaspoon chopped fresh cilantro (also known as coriander or Chinese parsley)
  2 medium avocados
  1 medium tomato, peeled, seeded and chopped
  2 tablespoons finely minced onion
  1 teaspoon chopped fresh cilantro
  1 garlic clove, minced

Combine first 3 ingredients with salt in blender and mix to smooth paste. Transfer to serving bowl. Peel and seed avocados. Add to chili paste, mashing coarsely with fork. Blend in remaining ingredients.

Garnish with additional chopped tomato and onion if using as a dip.

🦐 EGG ROLLS 🦐

There are two Egg Roll recipes in this collection simply because they are both good and I couldn't decide which one was best.

Makes about 16 egg rolls.

- 1 pound ground pork
- 3 cups finely shredded cabbage
- 1 8½-ounce can bamboo shoots, drained and chopped
- ½ cup chopped mushrooms
- 4 medium green onions, chopped
- 2 tablespoons soy sauce
- 1 teaspoon cornstarch
- 1 teaspoon salt
- ½ teaspoon sugar
- 1 pound egg roll wrappers (or spring roll wrappers)*
- Vegetable oil for frying

Stir-fry pork in wok or 10-inch skillet until brown. Remove pork from wok; drain, reserving 2 tablespoons fat. Stir-fry cabbage, bamboo shoots, mushrooms and onions in reserved fat. Mix soy sauce, cornstarch, salt and sugar; pour over vegetable mixture. Stir-fry 1 minute; cool. Mix pork and vegetables.

Place ½ cup pork mixture on center of each egg roll skin. Fold one corner of egg roll wrapper over filling. Overlap the two opposite corners. Moisten fourth corner with water; fold over to make into roll.

Heat vegetable oil in wok or large skillet (1½ to 1¾ inches) to 350°F (hot). Fry 3 to 5 egg rolls at a time until golden brown, turning once, about 3 minutes per side. Drain on paper towels. Serve with sweet and sour sauce or hot mustard sauce. See Fried Shrimp Wonton for these sauce recipes.

*Egg roll skins (or wrappers) can be found in the fresh vegetable section of your grocery store or at any oriental market. The wrappers dry out quickly when they are left unwrapped. Keep them covered with a damp towel to keep them soft.

🍄 EGG ROLLS WITH SHRIMP 🍄

Makes about 16 egg rolls.

- 1/2 pound raw shrimp
- 1/2 pound fresh bean sprouts
- 3 tablespoons oil, divided
- 1/2 pound ground pork
- 1 tablespoon Chinese rice wine or dry sherry
- 1 tablespoon soy sauce
- 1/2 teaspoon sugar
- 2 to 3 medium-size fresh mushrooms, finely chopped
- 2 cups finely chopped celery
- 1 teaspoon salt
- 1 tablespoon cornstarch, dissolved in 2 tablespoons chicken broth
- Egg roll wrappers (see note from previous Egg Rolls recipe)
- Vegetable oil for frying

Clean and de-vein shrimp. Cut shrimp into fine dice. Rinse bean sprouts in cold water and discard any husks that float to the top. Drain and pat them dry with paper towels.

Heat 1 tablespoon oil in wok or large skillet. Add the pork and stir-fry for 2 minutes or until it loses its reddish color. Add the wine, soy sauce, sugar, shrimp and mushrooms and stir-fry for another minute or until the shrimp turn pink. Transfer the entire contents of the pan to a bowl and set aside.

Add the remaining 2 tablespoons of oil into the same wok or skillet and heat 30 seconds. Add the celery and stir-fry for 5 minutes, then add the salt and bean sprouts and mix thoroughly together. Return pork and shrimp mixture to the pan and stir until all ingredients are well combined. Cook over moderate heat, stirring constantly until the liquid begins to boil.

There should be about 2 to 3 tablespoons of liquid remaining in the pan. If there is more, spoon it out and discard it. Give the cornstarch mixture a quick stir and add it to the mixture, stirring until the liquid is slightly thickened.

Place ½ cup of the mixture on the center of each egg roll wrapper. Fold one corner of the skin over the filling. Overlap the two opposite corners. Moisten the fourth corner with water; fold over to make a roll.

Heat oil 1½ inches deep in wok to 350°F (hot). Fry 3 to 5 egg rolls at a time until golden brown, turning once, about 3 minutes per side. Drain on paper towels. Serve with sweet and sour sauce or hot mustard sauce. See Fried Shrimp Wonton for these sauce recipes.

🦌 FRIED SHRIMP WONTON 🦌

These are not difficult to make but they are time consuming. This recipe makes about 60 wonton. They freeze very well and keep in the freezer for 2 to 3 months. Freeze them on a cookie sheet (before frying), then transfer them to a plastic bag for storage.

Makes about 60 wonton.

- 4 ounces ground pork
- 6 to 8 ounces raw shrimp, cleaned and finely chopped
- 2 tablespoons chicken broth
- 1 green onion, finely chopped
- 3/4 teaspoon salt
- 1 package wonton wrappers*

Mix pork, shrimp, broth, green onion and salt. Moisten edges of the wonton wrapper**, using a small pastry brush. Place about 1/2 tablespoon filling in the center of the wrapper. Fold one corner to opposite corner to form triangle. Moisten the corners of the triangle and fold the corners over one another. Deep fry in hot oil until golden. Serve with sweet and sour sauce or hot mustard sauce. Sauce recipes follow.

*Wonton wrappers can be found in the fresh vegetable section of your grocery store or in an oriental store.

**Keep wonton wrappers covered with a damp cloth to prevent drying before use.

HOT MUSTARD SAUCE:

Mix dry mustard with water to desired consistency. This is a very hot sauce, so be careful.

SWEET AND SOUR SAUCE:

    1 cup water
    3 tablespoons apricot preserves
    5 tablespoons white vinegar
    2 teaspoons catsup
    7 tablespoons sugar
    3 or 4 teaspoons cornstarch, mixed with 1 tablespoon water

Mix all ingredients together well. Cook over high heat in a small saucepan until boiling. Remove from heat. Cool.

Appetizers and Snacks

🦌 CHICKEN PILLOWS 🦌

When I had made what I thought was my final selection of the recipes to be included in this collection, I discussed the choices with some of my young friends. They said, "Oh, you didn't include your Chicken Pillows!" So here they are.

These are crisp and garlicky pastries that can be put together way ahead of time and frozen. Remove from your freezer just before baking.

Makes about 24 pastries.

- 2 whole chicken breasts, halved, skinned and boned
- 3 tablespoons lemon juice
- 2 tablespoons olive oil or vegetable oil
- 1 teaspoon finely chopped garlic
- 1 teaspoon crumbled leaf oregano
- 1 teaspoon salt
- 1/2 cup (1 stick) butter
- 1/2 pound phyllo or strudel pastry leaves*
- Waxed paper

Preheat oven to 400°F.

Cut the chicken into 1-inch pieces.

Combine lemon juice, oil, garlic, oregano and salt in a small bowl; mix well. Add the chicken pieces and coat with the marinade. Cover and refrigerate overnight.

Melt butter over low heat. Unwrap phyllo and place on a piece of wax paper. Keep phyllo covered with another piece of wax paper at all times to prevent drying out. Halve the phyllo dough lengthwise with scissors, forming 2 long strips, about 6 inches wide. Take one strip of phyllo, fold in half crosswise and brush with butter.

Place 2 pieces of chicken at one short end and roll up in pastry to the midpoint. Fold left and right edges toward the center over filling and continue rolling, forming a neat package. Brush tops and sides with butter and place seam-side down on a jelly-roll pan. Repeat with remaining chicken and phyllo.

Bake for 15 minutes or until golden brown.

NOTE: When I make these I always double the recipe. They are not complicated, but they do take time and I feel that if I'm going to make some, I might as well make a lot. They will keep for quite a long time in the freezer.

TO FREEZE AHEAD: Place filled and buttered phyllo rolls on a large baking sheet and freeze. When frozen, transfer to a large plastic bag and seal. To bake, place rolls in a single layer on a jelly-roll pan; brush tops and sides again with additional butter. Bake in a hot oven (400°F) for 20 minutes.

*Phyllo dough can be found in the frozen food section of your grocery store.

Appetizers and Snacks

❦ CLAM APPETIZERS ❦

These things are so delicious that I could not leave them out. Your local fish market will probably have some clam shells they will give you.

Makes 15 to 20 appetizers, according to size of clam shells.

- 3/4 cup finely chopped onion
- 3/4 cup finely chopped green pepper
- 2 tablespoons butter
- 1 teaspoon dried parsley
- 1 tablespoon plus 2 drops lemon juice (overflowing tablespoon)
- 2 1/2 teaspoons Worcestershire sauce
- 3 shakes Tabasco
- 1 can clams, including juice
- Progresso bread crumbs, approximately 1 cup
- Paprika
- Clam shells

Preheat oven to 425°F.

Cook onion and green pepper in butter until soft. Add parsley, lemon juice, Worcestershire sauce and Tabasco and simmer for a few minutes. Add clams and let it come to a boil and then simmer for about five minutes more. Remove from heat. Add approximately 1 cup Progresso bread crumbs. Let this thicken and stand for a few minutes. Fill clam shells with this mixture. Sprinkle a few bread crumbs on top of each shell. Sprinkle each shell with paprika.

Bake for about 20 minutes.

❦ HOT CRABMEAT CANAPES ❦

Crabmeat is so darned expensive! Now there is an imitation crabmeat on the market. It is pretty good but not AS good. Of course, you can always use the real thing.

Makes about 30 appetizers.

- 3 tablespoons butter, melted
- 3 tablespoons flour
- 1/2 teaspoon salt
- 1/4 teaspoon pepper
- 1 cup whipping cream
- 1 egg yolk
- 1/4 cup sherry
- 8 ounces cooked crabmeat, chopped fine
- 30 rounds melba toast or toasted bread
- 2 1/2 tablespoons grated Parmesan cheese

Blend butter, flour, salt and pepper in saucepan. Gradually add cream and, over low heat, cook until mixture thickens, stirring constantly.

Mix egg yolk and sherry together. Stir some of the hot mixture into the egg yolk mixture and then stir egg yolk mixture into the cream sauce. Mix in crabmeat. Top each toasted round with the mixture, sprinkle with grated cheese and place under the broiler briefly to heat through. Serve immediately.

Appetizers and Snacks

❧ PARTY SAUSAGE BISCUITS ❧

Makes 100 biscuits, but they may be frozen and heated in the oven before serving.

- 1 pound sharp cheese, grated
- 1 pound hot bulk sausage
- 3 cups Bisquick baking mix
- Water

Preheat oven to 400°F.

Let the cheese and sausage come to room temperature. Mix the sausage, cheese and biscuit mix. Add a little water if too dry. Form into walnut size balls, place on an *ungreased* cookie sheet and flatten. Bake for 10 minutes.

❧ ALOHA CRISPS ❧

Sweet and smokey flavors blend with crisp and juicy textures for these sensational treats. This recipe will make about 16 crisps, but you can make as many as you like. Just use a larger can of pineapple and more bacon.

- $1^{1}/_{3}$ cups (13-ounce can) pineapple chunks, drained
- $1/2$ pound (about 8 strips) bacon, halved or cut into thirds
- Wooden toothpicks

Preheat broiler. Wrap one piece of bacon around each pineapple chunk; secure with a wooden toothpick. Broil 5 to 8 minutes, until bacon is crisp. Serve hot.

❦ DEVILED HAM SPREAD ❦

You do need a food processor for this recipe, but it is a great way to use up leftover ham. Good on sandwiches or as a cocktail spread.

Makes about 2 cups.

- 1 small onion, peeled and quartered
- 1/2 pound cooked, smoked ham, cut into 1-inch cubes
- 2 tablespoons Dijon mustard
- 3 tablespoons mayonnaise
- 2 tablespoons milk or light cream
- 1/4 teaspoon cayenne pepper

Place all ingredients in a food processor fitted with the metal chopper blade. Turn on the motor and let run 15 seconds non-stop. Uncover the work bowl, scrape the sides of the bowl down with a rubber spatula, recover and run 15 seconds longer or until uniformly smooth and creamy.

❦ CRACKER SPREAD ❦

This is quick and easy to make when you have unexpected guests.

Makes about 2 cups.

- 1 tablespoon onion, diced
- 1 tablespoon dry vermouth
- 1 tablespoon mayonnaise
- 1 8-ounce package cream cheese, softened
- 1 3-ounce package dried beef
- 1/4 cup chopped stuffed green olives
- Assorted crackers

Add onion, vermouth and mayonnaise to the cream cheese. Cut dried beef with scissors to dice; add to cheese mixture. Add olives. Dilute with more vermouth if necessary.

Appetizers and Snacks

❧ SURPRISE CHEESE PUFFS ❧

The original recipe called for stuffed green olives, but we thought they were too salty and now use pitted black olives.

Makes about 50 appetizers.

- 1/2 cup butter
- 2 cups grated sharp cheese
- 1/2 teaspoon salt
- 1 teaspoon paprika
- Dash cayenne or red pepper
- 1 cup all-purpose flour
- 50 small ripe pitted olives

Preheat oven to 400°F.

Allow butter to soften; blend in cheese, salt, paprika and cayenne. Stir in flour, mixing well. Mold 1 teaspoon of this mixture around each olive, covering completely. Arrange on a baking sheet and chill until firm. Bake for 15 minutes. Serve hot.

NOTE: These little puffs are so easy to serve at parties since they may be made in advance, frozen on a baking sheet, then placed in a plastic bag and stored in the freezer. Just bake as needed.

🌶 MARINATED MUSHROOMS 🌶

These are so easy and so good. They will keep 2 to 3 weeks in the refrigerator. Mushrooms will turn a little dark, so don't be alarmed.

- 1/3 cup tarragon vinegar
- 1 package Good Seasons Italian dressing mix
- 6 drops Tabasco sauce
- 2/3 cups salad oil
- 1 tablespoon sugar
- 4 garlic cloves
- 2 tablespoons water
- 1 medium onion, sliced and separated into rings
- 1 pound fresh mushrooms (medium size)

Place all ingredients except onions and mushrooms in blender or food processor and blend well. If you do not have a blender or food processor, you can mince the garlic and shake ingredients in a closed jar. Pour over mushrooms and onions and marinade for at least 24 hours.

❧ REUBEN APPETIZERS ❧

If you like Reuben sandwiches, you'll love these.

Makes about 30 appetizers.

    1 loaf (about 30 slices) party rye bread
    1/2 pound corned beef, thinly sliced
    1 8-ounce can (1 cup) sauerkraut, well drained*
    1/4 cup Thousand Island dressing
    8 slices processed Swiss cheese, cut into fourths
    Cherry tomatoes, halved (garnish - optional)

Preheat broiler.

Place bread slices on cookie sheet. Top with corned beef, then sauerkraut, salad dressing and cheese. Broil about 6 inches away from heat for 2 to 3 minutes or until cheese melts. Garnish with cherry tomatoes.

*For thoroughly drained sauerkraut, drain liquid and place sauerkraut in 2 to 3 layers of paper towels; squeeze out the excess liquid.

❦ MEOW MIX ❦

When my oldest son was in college, I sent this to him in a care package. When his friends learned that the containers I used had at one time contained dried cat food, they immediately dubbed it "Meow Mix".

You can use peanuts, pretzels or any other such thing that you would like in this recipe.

    1 1/2 sticks unsalted butter (no margarine, please)
    3 to 4 tablespoons Worcestershire sauce
    1 10-ounce box Corn Chex
    1/2 10-ounce box Cheerios
    1/2 pound small pecan halves
        Garlic salt

Preheat oven to 250°F.

Melt butter. Mix Worcestershire sauce with butter and pour over combined Corn Chex, Cheerios and pecans, slowly, mixing well, being sure that all is coated. Salt to taste with garlic salt, again being sure that all is coated. Bake about 2 hours or until pecans are well toasted. Stir several times while baking.

NOTE: I use a large roasting pan to cook this in.

CHILE CON QUESO

Ladle over crisp tortillas or serve from a chafing dish as a dip for tortilla chips.

This makes about 4 cups, so cut the recipe in half if you need less.

- 1 tablespoon vegetable oil
- 1 large onion, chopped
- 1 garlic clove, minced
- 1 tablespoon all-purpose flour
- 1 tablespoon chili powder (or to taste)
- 1 10-ounce can tomatoes and green chiles
- 1 pound processed American cheese, cut into 1-inch cubes
- 2 jalapeno peppers (or to taste), seeded and finely chopped

Heat oil in 3-quart saucepan over medium heat. Add onion and garlic and saute until onion is translucent, about 5 minutes. Stir in flour and chili powder and cook, stirring constantly, 1 minute. Add tomatoes and chiles and continue cooking until thickened, about 5 or 6 minutes. Reduce heat to low and gradually add cheese, stirring constantly until cheese is completely melted. Stir in peppers. Taste and adjust seasonings. Serve hot.

🌶 TEX-MEX DIP 🌶

This seems to have originated in Texas, but it has appeared in several magazines. It deserves all the good publicity it has received. Be sure you have a crowd to help eat this - it makes quite a platter full.

```
3    medium-size ripe avocados
2    tablespoons lemon juice
1/2  teaspoon salt
1/4  teaspoon pepper
1    cup (8-ounces) sour cream
1/2  cup mayonnaise or salad dressing
1    package taco seasoning mix
2    10 1/2-ounce cans plain or jalapeno-flavored
     bean dip
1    large bunch green onions with tops, chopped
     (1 cup)
3    medium sized tomatoes, cored, halved and
     seeded
2    3 1/2-ounce cans pitted ripe olives, drained
     and coarsely chopped
8    ounces sharp Cheddar cheese, grated
     Large round tortilla chips
```

Peel, pit and mash avocados in a medium-size bowl with lemon juice, salt and pepper.

Coarsely chop the tomatoes. Drain and coarsely chop the ripe olives. Combine sour cream, mayonnaise and taco seasoning mix in another bowl.

TO ASSEMBLE: Spread bean dip on a large, shallow serving platter; top with seasoned avocado mixture; layer with sour cream-taco mixture. Sprinkle with chopped onions, tomatoes and olives; cover with grated cheese. Serve chilled or at room temperature with round tortilla chips.

Appetizers and Snacks

🦌 KOREAN CHICKEN WINGS 🦌

This recipe came to me from one of my in-laws in Hawaii. Every time I serve these I am asked for the recipe. They are very simple to make, but no one will know that if you keep the recipe to yourself. We like them so well that we often have them for dinner. Served with Ham Fried Rice, it is a good, simple Oriental meal.

    2 pounds chicken wings
    Flour for dredging
    Oil for frying

Remove tips from wings and disjoint the other two pieces. (Save the wing tips to make chicken broth for some other recipe.) Dredge chicken wings in flour and fry until done. Dip in sauce and serve hot.

SAUCE:

Mix together the following ingredients:

    ¼ cup soy sauce
    2 cloves garlic, minced
    1 teaspoon crushed red pepper
    ¼ cup sugar
    1 tablespoon minced green onions
    1 teaspoon sesame seeds

You do not cook the sauce mixture.

❦ SAUSAGE TRIANGLES ❦

This recipe came from a little recipe book I found in Hawaii. It calls for Portuguese sausage (linguica), spiced Italian sausage or Mexican chorizo. They are delicious with any highly spiced sausage.

Makes 30 or so appetizers.

- 1/2 pound Cheddar cheese, grated
- 1/4 pound sausage (highly spiced), chopped
- 1 egg, slightly beaten
- Bread triangles, crust removed*

Blend cheese, sausage and egg in mixing bowl. Toast bread triangles on one side. Pile mixture on bread, untoasted side. Place under broiler until bubbly and hot, approximately 5 minutes.

NOTE: These may be frozen on a cookie sheet (before cooking), then transferred to a plastic bag and stored in the freezer. They will keep for months.

*To make the bread triangles, remove the crust from the bread, leaving a square of bread remaining. Cut the square diagonally to make 2 triangles, then cut the 2 triangles in two to make 4.

🍄 MUSHROOM-CHEESE APPETIZERS 🍄

The hit of the party - worth a little extra fuss.

Makes 35 appetizers.

- 2 cups Bisquick baking mix
- 1/2 cup cold water
- 1/4 pound bulk pork sausage
- 1/4 cup finely chopped green onions (with tops)
- 3/4 cup mayonnaise
- 35 medium mushrooms (about 1 pound)
- 2 cups shredded Cheddar cheese (about 8 ounces)
- Paprika

Heat oven to 350°F.

Grease oblong 13x9x2-inch pan. Mix baking mix and water until a soft dough forms; beat vigorously, 20 strokes. Press dough in bottom of pan with floured hands.

Cook and stir sausage in skillet until brown; drain. Mix sausage, onions and mayonnaise. Remove stems from mushrooms. Finely chop stems; stir into sausage mixture. Fill mushroom caps with sausage mixture. Place mushrooms in rows on dough in pan; sprinkle with cheese and paprika.

Cover pan loosely with aluminum foil. Bake 20 minutes; remove foil. Bake until cheese is bubbly, 5 to 10 minutes. Let stand 15 minutes; cut into pieces.

🌶 CHINESE FRIED WALNUTS 🌶

One year, near Christmas, I found this recipe (with slight variations) in no less than four of the leading cooking magazines. Since I was not in the mood to bake cookies to give our friends, I made these instead, put them in decorative jars and included the recipe. Now my friends make them and give them for gifts.

Makes about 4 cups.

- 6 cups water
- 4 cups walnuts
- 1/2 cup sugar
- Salad oil
- Salt

In a 4-quart saucepan, over high heat, heat water to boiling; add walnuts, heat to boiling again and cook 1 minute. Rinse walnuts under running hot water; drain. Wash saucepan and dry well.

In a large bowl, with rubber spatula, gently stir warm walnuts with sugar until sugar dissolves. (If necessary, let mixture stand 5 minutes to dissolve sugar.)

Meanwhile, in same saucepan over medium heat, heat about 1 inch salad oil to 350°F (hot). With slotted spoon, add about half of the walnuts to oil; fry 5 minutes or until golden, stirring often.

With a slotted spoon, place walnuts in coarse sieve over bowl or sink to drain; sprinkle very lightly with salt; toss lightly to keep walnuts from sticking together. Transfer to paper towels to cool.

Fry remaining walnuts and proceed as above.

Store in tightly covered containers. Will keep for 2 to 3 weeks.

Appetizers and Snacks

TIP: The walnuts have a tendency to stick to the paper towels. I put a sheet of waxed paper over the toweling and use another paper towel to move the walnuts around, absorbing as much oil as possible.

SALADS AND SALAD DRESSINGS

🍎

Any basic cookbook will have a very good selection of salad dressing recipes and some of the bottled commercial dressings are excellent. But the ones here are special!

🌸 BLUE CHEESE SALAD DRESSING 🌸

This recipe gets an excellent rating! It can also be used as a dip for vegetables.

Makes about 2½ cups.

In blender container blend together:

> 1 ounce blue cheese
> ⅛ cup buttermilk
> Pinch of garlic powder
> 1 or 2 drops Tabasco sauce
> ¼ teaspoon Worcestershire sauce

Add and blend in:

> 1 cup mayonnaise
> 1 cup sour cream

Stir in:

> 1 ounce more of blue cheese

Will keep 2 to 3 weeks in the refrigerator.

🌶 VINAIGRETTE DRESSING 🌶

Makes ¾ cup.

- ¼ cup red wine vinegar
- 1 small clove garlic, minced
- ½ teaspoon salt
- ¼ teaspoon pepper
- ½ teaspoon dry mustard
- ½ cup vegetable oil

Combine all ingredients except oil in blender; blend well. Slowly add oil in a stream, mixing until thickened.

This will keep 2 to 3 weeks in the refrigerator.

🌶 CREAMY PEPPER DRESSING 🌶

Makes about 3 cups.

- 2 cups mayonnaise
- ½ cup milk
- ¼ cup water
- 2 tablespoons freshly grated Parmesan cheese
- 1 tablespoon freshly ground pepper
- 1 tablespoon cider vinegar
- 1 teaspoon lemon juice
- 1 teaspoon finely chopped onion
- 1 teaspoon garlic salt
- Dash of Tabasco sauce
- Dash of Worcestershire sauce

Whisk all ingredients until well combined. Chill thoroughly before serving.

❦ BASIC FRENCH DRESSING ❦

Makes about 2 cups.

- 1/2 cup vinegar
- 1 1/2 cups salad oil
- 1/2 teaspoon dry mustard
- 1 slice of a small onion
- 1 1/2 teaspoons salt
- 2 teaspoons sugar
- 1/2 teaspoon paprika

Put all ingredients in blender container and whirl until emulsified for 30 seconds or so. Store in a covered jar in the refrigerator.

❦ CREAMY GARLIC DRESSING ❦

Makes about 1 cup.

- 1 cup cottage cheese
- 1/4 cup milk
- 1/4 teaspoon white pepper
- 2 garlic cloves
- 2 teaspoons prepared mustard
- 2 teaspoons lemon juice

Blend all ingredients in blender.

🦌 CAESAR'S SALAD 🦌

Great! If serving fewer people, save some for the next night. Do not add dressing, croutons or cheese until ready to serve.

Serves 6 to 9.

- 1/3 cup olive oil
- 2 garlic cloves, coarsely chopped
- 2 tablespoons plus 1/2 teaspoon lemon juice
- 1 tablespoon Worcestershire sauce
- 1/2 teaspoon salt
- 1/4 teaspoon black pepper
- 1 head Romaine lettuce
- 1 raw egg, lightly beaten
- 1/2 cup grated Parmesan cheese
- 1/4 cup crumbled blue cheese
- Croutons (recipe follows)
- 4 flat anchovy fillets (optional)

Put the olive oil and garlic into a small bowl and let stand for 30 minutes, then add lemon juice, Worcestershire sauce, salt and pepper. Beat with a fork to mix well.

Wash and dry lettuce. Tear the leaves into bite-size pieces and place them in a large salad bowl. Pour on the salad dressing and toss quickly. Add the egg, Parmesan cheese and blue cheese. Toss.

Lastly, sprinkle the croutons over the salad and arrange the anchovies decoratively across top.

PROCESSOR METHOD:

With a metal blade, finely chop four 1-inch cubes Parmesan cheese. Drop two 1-inch cubes of blue cheese through the feed tube; process 2 seconds. Remove and set aside. Turn on machine; drop garlic through feed tube. Follow with oil, lemon juice, Worcestershire sauce, salt and pepper. Process 20 seconds. Add egg and turn off immediately.

CROUTONS:

**4 slices firm-textured white bread
Vegetable oil**

Trim the crust from the bread and cut the slices into ½-inch cubes. Pour oil into a large skillet to a depth of ½-inch. Heat the oil to a temperature of 350°F (hot). Add the bread cubes and fry over medium heat until crisp and golden. Remove the croutons from the skillet with a slotted spoon and drain well on paper towels. If you do not have a thermometer to check the temperature of the oil, put a bread cube in the hot oil and if it sizzles, the oil is hot enough.

❧ GREEK SALAD ❧

This big, beautiful, traditional salad makes a colorful addition to the supper menu. It is an easy, make-ahead salad if you save the dressing for a last-minute addition.

Serves 6.

- 1 head lettuce, separated into leaves
- 1 cucumber, thinly sliced
- 4 small, ripe tomatoes, cut into wedges
- 1 large red onion, sliced into rings
- 1/2 cup sliced radishes
- 1 cup (4 ounces) crumbled Feta cheese
- 12 Greek olives
- 1 tablespoon capers
- Greek dressing (recipe follows)

Line large, shallow salad bowl or platter with lettuce. Arrange ingredients neatly in sections; refrigerate several hours to chill thoroughly. Prepare Greek dressing. Refrigerate.

When ready to serve, pour dressing over salad; toss gently to coat all ingredients with dressing.

GREEK DRESSING:

- 1 teaspoon oregano, crumbled
- 1/2 cup olive oil
- 2 tablespoons cider vinegar
- 1/2 teaspoon dry mustard
- 1/2 teaspoon salt
- 1/8 teaspoon black pepper
- 1 2 ounce can anchovy fillets, drained and chopped (optional)

Combine all ingredients in a screw-top jar; shake to blend. Makes 2/3 cup.

🦌 CONCORDE SALAD 🦌

This tangy salad improves on standing in the refrigerator.

Serves 4 to 6.

- 1 1-pound can French-style green beans
- 1 1 pound can tiny peas
- 4 stalks celery, chopped (2 cups)
- 1/2 cup chopped green pepper
- 1 4-ounce jar pimentos, diced
- 1 medium-sized onion, sliced into rings
- 1/2 to 1 cup sugar*
- 3/4 cup cider vinegar
- 1/2 cup vegetable oil
- 1 teaspoon salt

Drain beans and peas and combine with celery, green pepper, pimento and onion in a large bowl. Stir sugar, vinegar, oil and salt together in a 2-cup measure until sugar is dissolved. Pour mixture over vegetables; stir gently. Refrigerate 24 hours. Drain off liquid 30 minutes before serving.

*For a less sweet salad, use the smaller amount of sugar.

🦌 TOSSED SALADS 🦌

Tossed salads cover a multitude of things. You can use just one lettuce, any kind or other greens, such as spinach. I like to mix the greens, that is, Iceberg, Bibb, Boston, Romaine, leaf lettuce, spinach and so on. Not all in one salad, of course, but any combination is fine.

Now you can add any combination of the following:

> **Thin sliced onion rings**
> **Cucumbers, sliced thin**
> **Sliced carrots**
> **Marinated artichokes**
> **Black or green olives, pitted**
> **Julienned ham, chicken and cheese**
> **Chopped green onions**
> **Beet slices, canned, drained**
> **Canned garbanzo beans, drained**
> **Radishes**
> **Green pepper, chopped or sliced**

Garnish with any of the following:

> **Tomatoes, chopped, sliced or cut into wedges**
> **Bacon, cooked and crumbled**
> **Chinese rice noodles**
> **Sunflower seeds**
> **Hard boiled eggs, sliced or chopped**
> **Croutons**
> **Grated cheese**

You can mix the greens, then put the other ingredients you are going to use in separate dishes and let everyone add what they like on their salad. You can use a good commercial salad dressing, make your own or use any of the dressings in this chapter.

❦ CHEF'S SALAD BOWL ❦

A great luncheon salad. Serve with bread, bread sticks or crackers.

Makes 6 servings.

CREAMY DRESSING:

- 1 8-ounce bottle herb-garlic dressing (Italian)
- 1/4 cup mayonnaise
- 1/4 teaspoon sugar

In small bowl, combine all dressing ingredients; with wire whisk or rotary beater, beat well. Refrigerate, covered.

SALAD:

- 1 1/2 quarts bite-size pieces crisp salad greens
- 2 tablespoons snipped chives (fresh, please), omit if fresh chives are not available
- 2 cups cooked, slivered ham (1/2 pound)
- 1 1/2 cups cooked and slivered chicken (1/2 pound)
- 1/2 pound natural Swiss cheese, slivered
- 2 medium tomatoes, cut into wedges

Just before serving, make salad. Place greens and chives in a salad bowl. Add ham, chicken and cheese.

Stir dressing well; pour over salad. Toss to coat meat and greens. Garnish with tomato wedges.

🦌 SUMMER'S BEST GREEN SALAD 🦌

You will notice that there is no oil in this salad dressing, therefore there are only about 40 calories in each serving.

Serves 6.

- 1 small head Romaine lettuce
- 1 small head leaf lettuce
- 3 green onions, sliced
- 1 envelope Good Seasons French dressing mix
- 3/4 cup tomato juice
- 1/4 cup cider vinegar
- 2 tablespoons water

Tear lettuce into bite-size pieces in large bowl. Add onions. Combine salad dressing mix, tomato juice, vinegar and water in a jar with a tight fitting lid; shake well to mix. Drizzle about 1/4 cup over the greens; toss to coat well. Pass the remaining dressing separately, if you wish.

❦ ORIENT EXPRESS CHICKEN SALAD ❦

This may be served on the Orient Express. I found it in one of my food magazines. I did take a few liberties and have written it as I served it.

Serves 6 to 8.

- 1 quart water
- 3 whole chicken breasts, split
- 3/4 cup mayonnaise
- 3/4 cup sour cream
- 2 apples, cored and diced
- 1 cup diced celery
- 1 cup slivered almonds, toasted
- 1/3 cup raisins, plumped in warm water, about 30 minutes
- 1 bunch parsley, chopped (1 to 1 1/2 cups, packed)
- Juice of 1 lemon
- Salt and freshly ground pepper
- 1 head Bibb or Boston lettuce, separated into leaves
- 1 tomato, thinly sliced

Bring water to boil. Add chicken breasts, reduce heat and poach until chicken is just cooked, about 10 minutes. Remove chicken and let cool (if you want, reserve stock for another recipe). Discard bones and skin; cut meat into 1/2-inch pieces. Combine chicken, mayonnaise, sour cream, apples, celery, almonds, raisins, parsley and lemon juice. Season with salt and pepper. Cover and refrigerate until ready to serve.

Arrange lettuce and tomato on platter. Top with salad.

🌱 TOMATO AND CHICK PEA SALAD 🌱

Where this came from, I do not know. But it is a great salad and improves on standing. A great make-ahead salad.

Serves 4 to 6.

       Red Wine Vinegar Dressing (recipe follows)
- 4 medium-sized tomatoes, peeled, seeded and chopped
- 1½ cups chopped celery
- 1 medium-sized cucumber, pared, seeded and chopped
- 1 green pepper, halved, seeded and chopped
- 1 sweet red pepper, halved, seeded and chopped
- 1 large onion, chopped (1 cup)
- 1 16-ounce can chick peas (garbanzos), drained
  Salad greens
  Dill or parsley sprigs for garnish

Prepare Red Wine Vinegar Dressing; set aside.

Combine tomatoes, celery, cucumber, green and red peppers, onion and chick peas in a large bowl. Pour dressing over; mix gently. Cover; refrigerate overnight or for up to 4 days.

TO SERVE: Drain dressing from salad and reserve for other salads. Spoon marinated vegetables into chilled salad bowl lined with salad greens. Garnish with dill or parsley sprigs, if you wish.

RED WINE VINEGAR DRESSING:

- $1/2$ cup red wine vinegar
- $1 1/2$ cups vegetable oil
- 1 tablespoon Dijon mustard
- Dash of Tabasco
- 3 cloves garlic, finely chopped
- $1/4$ cup chopped fresh dill or 1 tablespoon dried dillweed
- 2 teaspoons salt
- $1/2$ teaspoon pepper

Combine all ingredients in a large jar with a screw-top. Shake vigorously to blend. Makes about $2 1/4$ cups.

🦌 CAULIFLOWER SALAD 🦌

I first got this recipe from a friend in St. Louis about 15 years ago. Years later another friend in Detroit served it, but not from my recipe. In the August, 1982 issue of a first class gourmet magazine it was featured just as it is written here, except they called it "Surprise Salad" and they mixed the sugar, Parmesan cheese and mayonnaise before spreading it over the salad. It proves that good recipes get around.

Serves 10 to 12, but you can cut it down to size. Just cut all of the ingredients in half.

- 1 head lettuce, washed, dried and broken up
- 1 large red onion, sliced into rings
- 1 pound bacon, fried and broken into small pieces
- 1 head cauliflower, cut into bite-size pieces
- 1/4 cup sugar
- 1/3 cup grated Parmesan cheese
- Salt and pepper to taste
- 2 cups mayonnaise

Prepare night before in large bowl loosely (meaning do not pack down). 1st layer - lettuce, 2nd layer - onion, 3rd layer - bacon, 4th layer - cauliflower. There is only one layer of each of these.

Spread sugar, cheese, salt and pepper over top and then put mayonnaise on in spoonfuls. Cover and refrigerate overnight. Toss just before serving.

🐭 A VERY SPECIAL SPINACH SALAD 🐭

Serves 10 to 12.

- 1 10-ounce package fresh spinach, cleaned and broken up
- 1 head iceberg lettuce, cleaned and broken up
- 1 can sliced water chestnuts, drained
- 3 hard boiled eggs, sliced
- 3 tomatoes, quartered
- 1 can Chinese rice noodles*
- 7 slices bacon, fried crisp and crumbled

DRESSING:

- 3/4 cup sugar
- 1 cup salad oil
- 1 medium onion
- 1/2 cup red wine vinegar
- 1 tablespoon Worcestershire sauce
- 1 teaspoon salt
- 1/3 cup catsup

For the dressing, put ingredients in blender or processor and blend well.

Mix spinach, lettuce, chestnuts, eggs and tomatoes. Just before serving add dressing. Toss well. Sprinkle noodles and bacon on top and serve.

*Not chow mein noodles. Look for canned rice noodles in the Chinese section of your supermarket.

❦ RED CABBAGE COLESLAW ❦

Serves 12, but you can cut it down to size.

- 1 large head of red cabbage, shredded
- 1 pound large carrots, grated coarse
- 4 stalks of celery, cut into 1½-inch julienne strips
- 1 bunch of scallions, cut into 1½-inch julienne strips
- ⅓ cup fresh lemon juice
- ¼ cup cider vinegar
- 1½ tablespoons Dijon mustard
- 1 cup vegetable oil
- 1 tablespoon celery seed

In a large bowl toss the cabbage with carrots, celery and scallions. In a blender or food processor blend the lemon juice, vinegar and mustard. With the motor running, add the oil in a stream and blend the dressing until it is emulsified. Add the celery seeds and salt and pepper to taste. Pour the dressing over the salad and toss the salad well. Chill the salad, covered, for up to 3 hours.

❧ BONNIE'S POTATO SALAD ❧

There are literally thousands of recipes for potato salad. After trying at least five hundred, I compiled, tested, tasted and varied until I came up with this. You can create your own version by doing the same thing. All ingredients are approximate and can be adjusted to suit your taste. Can be halved or doubled.

Serves 8 to 10.

- 3 pounds boiling potatoes (NOT Idahos or Russets)
- 8 to 10 eggs, hard boiled
- 3/4 cup chopped onion
- 3/4 cup chopped sweet pickles or sweet pickle relish
- 1/4 cup chopped pimento
- 1 teaspoon or more celery seeds
- Salt to taste
- 1 cup Kraft's* mayonnaise or enough for desired consistency

Scrub and boil potatoes in skins until easily pierced with a fork. Peel and dice potatoes. Peel and dice hard boiled eggs. Combine and add all other ingredients, mix well.

*This is my favorite brand but you can use what you like best. Now don't yell at me if it isn't as good as you thought it would be. Try it using Kraft's!

❦ FRENCH POTATO SALAD ❦

This recipe was in a local newspaper. When you are asked to bring the potato salad, try this one. It is different and delicious. It does take a little time, but the compliments you will receive will make your efforts worthwhile.

Serves 8 to 10.

- 1 pound sliced bacon
- 3 pounds small, new red potatoes, unpeeled and cut into 1/4-inch slices
- 1 pound fresh green beans
- Salt
- Boiling water

DRESSING:

- 1/2 cup olive oil
- 1/4 cup canned, undiluted beef broth
- 1/4 cup chopped fresh parsley
- 1 teaspoon salt
- 1/2 teaspoon dried sweet basil
- Black pepper
- 1/4 cup tarragon vinegar
- 1/2 cup chopped green onions
- 1 garlic clove, crushed
- 1 teaspoon dry mustard
- 1/2 teaspoon dried tarragon

Cut bacon into 1 1/2-inch pieces (do not separate the strips, they will come apart while cooking). Place in large skillet. Cook bacon over medium heat until lightly browned, stirring occasionally, about 15 minutes. With slotted spoon, remove bacon to paper towels to drain. Save bacon drippings for another use or discard.

Place potatoes in pot or saucepan with salted, boiling water to cover; heat to a second boil. Cover and reduce heat; cook for 8 to 10 minutes or until the potatoes are fork-tender. Drain.

Meanwhile, wash and trim the green beans. Cut or break into 2-inch pieces. Place in another saucepan with about ½ inch of boiling water (salted). Cover and cook until tender-crisp, about 8 to 10 minutes. Drain.

FOR DRESSING: Combine all dressing ingredients and stir until well mixed. Set aside.

Combine potatoes and beans in a large bowl. Pour dressing mixture over warm vegetables, add drained bacon pieces and toss gently until well mixed. The liquid will be absorbed by the potatoes.

You can serve immediately, but it is best when left to marinade for 3 hours or so at room temperature. Always serve at room temperature.

❦ NEW POTATO SALAD WITH HERBS AND SHALLOTS ❦

Warm potatoes are tossed with shallots and a vinaigrette in this easy-to-make dish. It should be served at room temperature.

Makes 12 servings.

VINAIGRETTE:

- 3 tablespoons tarragon vinegar
- 1 teaspoon Dijon mustard
- 1 garlic clove, minced
- 9 tablespoons olive oil
- Salt and pepper

SALAD:

- 5 pounds new potatoes
- 3 shallots or green onions, minced
- 1 cup mayonnaise
- 1 cup diced celery
- 3/4 cup chopped green onions
- 1/4 cup chopped fresh dill or 1 tablespoon dried dillweed
- 3 tablespoons minced fresh parsley
- 2 tablespoons snipped fresh chives
- 3/4 pound bacon, fried crisp and broken up

FOR VINAIGRETTE: Combine vinegar, mustard and garlic in small bowl. Gradually whisk in oil. Season with salt and pepper.

FOR SALAD: Cover potatoes with salted water in large pot. Cover and boil gently until just tender. Drain. Cool slightly. Slice warm potatoes. Place in large bowl. Toss with vinaigrette and shallots. Let stand 30 minutes.

Mix mayonnaise, celery, green onions, dill, parsley, chives and bacon into potatoes. Adjust seasoning.

Can be prepared 1 day ahead. Cover and refrigerate. Bring to room temperature before serving.

SPAGHETTI SALAD

Generous servings for 8 to 10.

- 1 pound thin spaghetti, broken into thirds
- 4 green onions, diced
- 1 tomato, seeded and diced
- 1/2 seedless cucumber, diced
- 8 ounces commercial Italian dressing
- 2 tablespoons (or to taste) McCormick's Salad Supreme dressing*
- 2 to 3 tablespoons grated Parmesan cheese
- 1/4 cup sliced, pitted black olives
- 1/4 cup sliced green olives

Cook spaghetti according to package directions. Drain. Add all other ingredients. Mix and cool. Best when made one day in advance.

*This is found in the spice section of any grocery store.

❦ DILLED GREEN BEAN SALAD ❦

A good winter salad. Best when served with meat loaf or broiled fish.

Serves 4.

- 1 1-pound can cut green beans, drained
- 1/3 cup Caesar salad dressing (commercial or home made)
- 1 teaspoon dried dillweed
- 1/2 teaspoon marjoram

Combine drained green beans, Caesar salad dressing, dillweed and marjoram in a medium-sized bowl. Toss lightly together.

Cover with a plastic wrap. Chill in the refrigerator at least 3 hours. Serve in lettuce cups, if you wish.

Salads and Salad Dressings

❦ MARINATED STRING BEANS ❦

This is from one of the Ford Times cookbooks. That series of cookbooks is one of the best I have found. The recipes are from well known restaurants and most are very good. I've found some of the recipes do not make the conversion from restaurant quantities to home quantities very well, but most are excellent.

Serves 4 to 6.

- 2 1 pound cans cut green beans
- 1/3 cup sugar
- 2/3 teaspoon salt
- 2/3 cup cider vinegar
- 1/2 cup chopped onions
- Pinch of black pepper
- 1 tablespoon salad oil
- Lettuce

Drain beans, reserving 1/3 of the juice and discarding the remainder. Dissolve sugar and salt in the juice combined with the vinegar. Mix together beans, onions and black pepper, then pour on vinegar mixture. Add oil and stir gently to prevent beans from breaking. Chill overnight.

Serve on a bed of lettuce.

🍇 CUCUMBERS IN SOUR CREAM 🍇

Now, if you forget to start these a day in advance or at least several hours in advance, they are still good, but they will be somewhat watery if the cucumbers are not drained. Let the cucumbers and onions sit in the sour cream as long as possible. Thirty minutes is okay, 1 hour is better, etc.

Serves 4.

- 3 cucumbers, peeled and sliced very thin
  Salt
- 1 medium onion, peeled and sliced very thin
  Sour cream, approximately 1/2 to 2/3 cup

Place cucumbers in colander or sieve, salt and let sit for an hour or so to drain. Combine cucumbers and onions in a large bowl. Mix in enough sour cream to coat all cucumbers and onions. Cover and refrigerate several hours or overnight.

Salads and Salad Dressings

🌱 ROSOFF'S COLESLAW 🌱

This came from one of the leading gourmet magazines. The caption said it was unforgettable and they were right. I don't know how it got its name.

Makes about 7½ cups.

- 6 cups finely shredded cabbage (about 2¼ pounds)
- 1 cup thinly sliced Spanish onions
- 1/3 cup grated carrot
- 2/3 cup distilled white vinegar
- 1/4 cup minced sweet red pepper
- 3 tablespoons sugar
- 1/2 teaspoon salt
- 1/2 teaspoon pepper
- 2/3 cup vegetable oil

Combine cabbage, onion and carrot in a ceramic or glass bowl. Mix all remaining ingredients together well and pour over cabbage mixture. Mix well. Chill the coleslaw, covered, for at least 6 hours.

🌶 BUFFET BEAN SALAD 🌶

When I first bought my blender, I sent for the recipe book that they recommended. It was very helpful with the use of the blender and I also got a few very good recipes from it. This is one of them. Keeps for days and days in the refrigerator.

Makes 6 to 8 cups.

- 1/2 cup red wine vinegar
- 1/2 cup sugar
- 1/2 teaspoon coarse black pepper
- 1/2 cup salad oil
- 1 teaspoon salt
- 1 large onion, cut into pieces
- 1 green pepper, cut into pieces

Place the above ingredients in blender container and blend until all vegetables are chopped fine. Pour contents over:

- 1 can yellow wax beans, drained
- 1 can green beans, drained
- 1 can kidney beans, drained
  Any other canned beans may be used, such as garbanzos, limas or pintos.

Best when marinated for 24 hours.

Salads and Salad Dressings

❦ BLACKHAWK SALAD BOWL ❦

This came from one of the food magazines. It is probably from a restaurant, but I'm not sure. It is similar to Caesar's Salad, but different. An excellent luncheon salad.

Serves 6 to 8.

- 1 3-ounce package cream cheese, at room temperature
- 3 ounces blue cheese, crumbled
- 5 to 6 tablespoons water
- 1 egg
- 1 tablespoon plus 1½ teaspoons fresh lemon juice
- 1 cup vegetable oil, divided
- ¼ cup red wine vinegar
- 2 tablespoons mayonnaise
- 2 tablespoons chopped chives
- 1 tablespoon sugar
- 1½ teaspoons Worcestershire sauce
- ¾ teaspoon paprika
- ¾ teaspoon salt
- 1 clove garlic, crushed
- ¼ teaspoon prepared hot mustard
- ¼ teaspoon white pepper
- 8 cups torn salad greens
- 1 hard-cooked egg, chopped
- Seasoned salt
- Pepper
- 8 anchovy fillets (garnish)

Beat cheeses in small bowl until smooth. Beat in water, 1 tablespoon at a time, until mixture is pourable. Set aside.

Combine egg, lemon juice and ¼ cup oil in blender and mix on medium speed for 15 seconds. Increase speed to high and add remaining oil in a slow, steady stream, stopping occasionally to scrape down the sides of the container. Add vinegar, mayonnaise, chives, sugar, Worcestershire sauce, paprika, salt, garlic, mustard and white pepper and blend until smooth.

Combine salad greens in large bowl with enough dressing to coat. Sprinkle with chopped eggs and seasoned salt and toss gently. Add 2 to 3 tablespoons cheese mixture and pepper to taste and toss again. Add anchovies.

Remaining dressing and cheese mixture can be covered and kept in the refrigerator for up to 2 weeks.

❦ STRAWBERRY NUT SALAD ❦

This is a must at our house at holiday time. It goes best with turkey or ham. It makes enough to serve 12, but you can cut it in half. However, the leftovers have never gone to waste in my house.

- 1 6-ounce package strawberry Jello
- 1 cup boiling water
- 2 10-ounce packages frozen strawberries, thawed, undrained
- 1 20-ounce can crushed pineapple, drained
- 3 medium bananas, mashed
- 1 cup walnuts, chopped
- 1 pint sour cream

Combine Jello with 1 cup boiling water.and stir until Jello is completely dissolved. Fold in strawberries, pineapple, bananas and walnuts. Put half of the mixture in a 12x8x2-inch dish. Refrigerate until firm. Spread with sour cream. Top with the remaining mixture. Refrigerate again until firm. Cut into squares and serve on lettuce.

❦ STRAWBERRY SOUFFLE SALADS ❦

Very good. Best served with ham, pork or turkey.

Makes 4 to 6 servings.

- 1 10-ounce package frozen, sliced strawberries, thawed
- 1 3-ounce package strawberry Jello
- 1/4 teaspoon salt
- 1 cup boiling water
- 2 tablespoons lemon juice
- 1/4 cup mayonnaise
- 1/4 cup chopped walnuts
- Lettuce
- Canned pineapple slices

Drain berries, reserving liquid. Add enough water to liquid to make 3/4 cup. Dissolve Jello and salt in boiling water. Add reserved liquid and lemon juice. Beat in mayonnaise. Chill until partially set. Beat with an electric mixer until fluffy. Fold in berries and nuts. Pour into individual oiled molds. Chill until set. Unmold on lettuce-lined platter atop a slice of pineapple. Serve with additional mayonnaise.

🌰 WALDORF SALAD 🌰

Serves 6.

    1/2 cup walnuts
      3 large stalks celery
      6 medium apples
    1/2 cup raisins
    1/2 cup mayonnaise
        Lettuce

Slice walnuts, celery and apples. Mix together. Add raisins and mayonnaise and toss. Serve on lettuce leaves.

SOUPS AND STEWS

When you are planning your dinner menu, check this section. There is nothing better, especially during cold winter months, than a hot, hearty soup or stew with crusty garlic bread and a salad for dinner.

❦ SAUSAGE RAGOUT ❦

Made with both sweet and hot Italian sausage and red and green peppers, this hearty dish is suitable for any season, but is especially welcome in the the cold months.

Makes 6 to 8 servings.

- 2 to 4 tablespoons olive oil
- 1 1/2 pounds hot Italian sausage, cut into 2-inch pieces
- 1 1/2 pounds sweet Italian sausage, cut into 2-inch pieces
- 1 1/2 cups chopped onion
- 1 1/2 teaspoons minced garlic
- 2 cups diced (1-inch) red bell pepper
- 2 cups diced (1-inch) green bell pepper
- 1 28-ounce can Italian plum tomatoes
- 1/2 cup dry red wine
- 3/4 cup fresh Italian parsley, chopped and divided
- 2 1/2 tablespoons tomato paste
- Salt and pepper to taste

Heat 2 tablespoons oil in large skillet over medium heat until rippling. Brown sausage in batches, adding more oil if needed and removing sausage with slotted spoon as it is browned. Pour off all but 2 tablespoons drippings. Add onion and garlic to skillet; cook, stirring constantly and scraping brown bits from bottom of skillet, until onion is soft, 8 to 10 minutes. Stir in red and green peppers; cook, stirring occasionally, 5 minutes. Stir in tomatoes, wine, 1/2 cup of the parsley, tomato paste and salt and pepper to taste. Cook about 10 minutes. Combine sausage and vegetable mixture in Dutch oven; toss to mix well. Heat to boiling; reduce heat. Simmer, covered, 15 minutes. Uncover Dutch oven; cook, stirring occasionally, until peppers are tender, 15 to 20 minutes. Taste and adjust seasonings with salt and pepper. Sprinkle with remaining parsley.

❧ SOUTHWEST BEEF STEW ❧
Using Food Processor

It is a good idea to make this stew in advance, up to 3 days, so the flavors have a chance to marry. Serve it over hot, buttered noodles.

Serves 6 to 8.

- 4 large garlic cloves
- 2 medium onions, peeled and quartered
- 1 cup prepared chili sauce
- 1 tablespoon tomato paste
- 1 small chipotle chili*
- 2 pounds lean beef stew meat, cut into ¾-inch cubes
- 1 tablespoon ground cumin
- 1 teaspoon salt
- 3 tablespoons vegetable oil, divided
- 1 cup canned beef broth

Preheat oven to 350°F.

With steel blade in place in processor and machine running, drop garlic through feed tube and mince. Add onions and mince. Transfer to sheet of waxed paper. Process chili sauce, tomato paste and chipotle until smooth.

Combine beef with cumin and salt in large plastic bag. Close bag and toss well until meat cubes are uniformly seasoned. Heat ½ tablespoon oil in a heavy 3-quart stove-top-to-oven pot over medium-high heat. Brown meat in batches, adding more oil as necessary. Transfer to plate.

Add 1 tablespoon oil to pot; add garlic and onions. Cover with a sheet of waxed paper.** Cook over medium heat until soft, stirring occasionally to loosen any browned bits, about 6 minutes. Return meat to pot. Add chili sauce mixture and ¾ cup beef broth. Stir to combine. Cover and bake until tender, about 1½ hours, stirring occasionally and adding more broth as necessary to keep meat covered.

*Chipotle chilis are smoked jalapenos. You can usually find them in the Mexican food area of your local grocery store. If not, you can use any canned jalapenos.

**This procedure is a cross between sauteing and steaming. Lift the wax paper to stir and remove and discard before putting meat back into pot.

❦ LAZY DAY OVEN STEW ❦

This is just what the name implies. Put it in the oven, go shopping or whatever and your spouse will think you've slaved all day over a hot stove.

Serves 6 to 8.

- 2 pounds stew meat, cut into 1-inch pieces
- 2 onions, sliced
- 8 carrots, scraped and cut into chunks
- 6 potatoes, peeled and cut into chunks
- 2 stalks celery, cut diagonally
- 2 teaspoons salt
- 2 tablespoons sugar
- 1/4 cup Minute Tapioca
- 2 cups V-8 Juice or tomato juice
- 1/2 cup red wine

Preheat oven to 250°F.

Place meat in a large shallow pan (9x12) and cover with vegetables. Mix salt, sugar, tapioca, juice and red wine and pour over meat and vegetables. Cover tightly with aluminum foil and bake for 5 hours. Stir well before serving.

🌱 PORTUGUESE VEGETABLE SOUP 🌱

A good, hearty soup!

Serves 10 to 12.

- 4 cups water
- 1 small beef shank, cross-cut
- 1/2 cup dry, split peas
- 1/2 tablespoon salt
- 1 large clove garlic, minced
- 4 ounces Italian sausages, sliced
- 2 small to medium tomatoes, peeled, seeded and chopped
- 1 medium carrot, sliced thin
- 1/2 medium onion, chopped
- 1/4 medium green pepper, chopped
- 1/2 cup elbow macaroni

In a large kettle, combine water, beef shank, split peas, salt and garlic. Bring to a boil. Reduce heat; simmer, covered, for 1 hour. Remove beef shank. Cool until the meat can be easily handled. Cut meat off bone; discard bone. Dice meat and return to kettle. Add sausages, tomatoes, carrots, onion and green pepper. Simmer, covered, 20 minutes. Add macaroni. Simmer, covered, about 10 minutes longer.

❦ PLAZA III STEAK SOUP ❦

This recipe was published in one of those cookbooks that features recipes from famous restaurants. Since it was from a restaurant that I frequented when we lived in Missouri and I had eaten this soup for lunch numerous times, I was amazed when I tried the recipe. It was nothing like what I had eaten there. Hence, some changes. I do not know if it is exactly like the restaurant's, but I do know that it is superb. It is a meal in itself and freezes well.

Makes 2 quarts.

- 1 pound ground beef
- 1 stick butter (1/4 pound)
- 1 cup flour
- 5 cups water
- 1 teaspoon Ac'cent (optional)
- 1/2 teaspoon pepper
- 1 28-ounce can peeled tomatoes, chopped
- 2 tablespoons beef base*
- 1 tablespoon Kitchen Bouquet browning sauce
- 1/2 cup each of chopped onions, celery and carrots, *parboiled*
- 1 cup frozen mixed vegetables

Brown meat, drain and set aside. Melt butter in a 4-quart Dutch oven and whip in the flour, Ac'cent and pepper to make a smooth paste. Add water and whisk while heating to thicken. Add tomatoes and beef base, heat and stir well. Add browning sauce, rest of vegetables and cooked beef. Cook over medium heat for 30 minutes, stirring occasionally. Salt to taste.

*Beef base can be found in the spice rack at the grocery store. Be sure to refrigerate it after opening.

❦ VEGETABLE BEEF SOUP ❦

It took awhile, but I finally realized that most recipes are only a guide and need not be followed to a tee. The first time I use a recipe, I follow it as closely as possible. Except for breads and pastries, I now make each recipe my own. This recipe is a good one for you to do the same

Makes about 3 quarts.

- 1 28-ounce can tomatoes, chopped or mashed
- 1/2 pound inexpensive beef, such as beef shank
- 1 large soup bone (for additional flavor)
- 1 large onion, chopped
- 2 cans (your tomato can) water
- A little salt and pepper
- 1 heaping teaspoon dried parsley flakes

Put the above ingredients in a large pot (4 quarts or so) and bring to a boil. Lower heat to a low boil and cook until meat literally falls apart, about 2 hours, checking occasionally to see if you need more water. Remove and discard soup bone. Cut meat from beef shank into small pieces.

Now use your imagination! Some suggestions are:

- 2 potatoes, peeled and diced
- 1/2 cup fresh or frozen corn
- 1/2 cup green peas
- 1/2 cup diced celery
- 2 carrots, peeled and diced
- 1/2 cup green beans
- 1/2 cup shredded cabbage
- Left-over vegetables from your refrigerator

Add vegetables to tomato mixture and cook until vegetables are well done. Add more salt and pepper to taste. If you want the soup a little thicker, add a tablespoon or so of instant potatoes. Or better still, use left-over mashed potatoes, if you have them.

RED BEAN SOUP

This soup will be better if you add a little salt during cooking time and adjust to suit your taste when finished. Don't ask me why, it's just that way.

Serves 8 to 10.

- 1 pound kidney beans
- 1 large smoked ham hock
- 2 cloves garlic, minced
- Salt (Sea salt or Kosher salt preferred)
- 2 tablespoons tomato paste

Pick over beans to remove any withered or bad ones and to remove any stones which are sometimes found in dried beans. Rinse and put beans, ham hock and garlic in a 4 to 5-quart Dutch oven. Cover with water to three inches above beans. Bring to a boil, then reduce to a simmer or low heat. Cook for 2 to 3 hours or until the beans are well done. Check frequently and add more water as needed. Add tomato paste during the last hour of cooking.

Beans will hold their shape better and cook faster if soaked overnight in cold water, but we like them mushy.

❦ LENTIL SOUP WITH HAM ❦

Serves 6.

- 2 cups dried lentils
- 1/2 cup finely chopped onion
- 1/2 cup diced, cooked ham
- 1 to 1 1/2 teaspoons salt
- 1 ham bone (optional)
- 2 cloves garlic, minced
- 1 16-ounce can tomatoes, mashed
- 1/4 teaspoon ground pepper

Combine all ingredients in Dutch oven. Add cold water to cover by 3 inches. Heat to boiling; reduce heat. Simmer, uncovered, until lentils are tender, about 45 minutes.

WONTON SOUP

The recipe for the wonton, which precedes the recipe for the soup, makes about 60 wonton. You will need only 12 to 14 for the soup. Freeze the remaining wonton on a cookie sheet and then transfer to a plastic bag. You do not need to thaw them before you make your next soup.

Serves 4 to 6.

WONTON:

- 1/2 pound ground pork
- 1 tablespoon soy sauce
- 1 teaspoon chicken bouillon granules, dissolved in 2 tablespoons water
- 1 tablespoon sesame oil*
- 1/3 package frozen spinach, thawed and water squeezed out**
- 1 pound wonton wrappers***

Mix all ingredients, except wrappers, together. Moisten the edges of a wonton wrapper, using a pastry brush. Place 1 heaping teaspoon of filling on the center of the wrapper. Fold one corner to opposite corner to form triangle. Fold two remaining opposite corners to center, overlapping and pinch together. That's all there is to it.

Fill a three quart pot about two-thirds full with water. Bring to boil. Add wonton (about 12 to 14), stirring gently once. Cook 3 to 5 minutes until wonton float to surface. Sprinkle 1/4 cup cold water over wonton and bring to boil again. Now they are done. You cook the frozen wonton exactly the same way.

SOUP:

    3 cups chicken broth
    1/2 cup thin strips of Virginia ham or Canadian bacon
    2 cups sliced Romaine lettuce
    Salt to taste

Cook chicken broth and ham for 5 minutes on high heat. Add Romaine lettuce. Stir and remove pot from heat. Season to taste with salt. Add cooked wonton to soup and serve.

*Sesame oil can be found in the specialty section of your grocery store or in any Oriental store.

**Cut the frozen spinach into 3 equal sections. Freeze two sections and save for the next time you make wonton.

***You can find the wonton wrappers in the fresh vegetable section at the grocery store or in any Oriental store.

🌶 CHINESE EGG DROP SOUP 🌶

Serves 4 to 6.

    3 or 4 dried mushrooms*, soaked in hot water until soft
    4 cups chicken broth
    1 teaspoon chicken bouillon (granules)
1 1/2 teaspoons soy sauce
    2 tablespoons cornstarch, mixed with 2 tablespoons water
    1 or 2 eggs, beaten
    1 green onion, minced
1 1/2 teaspoons sesame oil*
    Dash of salt

Remove stems from mushrooms and discard. Chop mushrooms.

Bring chicken broth, bouillon, soy sauce and mushrooms to a boil. Remove from heat. Add cornstarch (mixed with the water) to the broth. Return pot to low heat. Pour in beaten eggs in a slow stream, holding the dish 12 to 14 inches above the soup pot as you pour and stir gently, but quickly, until the eggs set. Remove from heat. Add scallions and sesame oil, mix well. Season to taste with salt and serve.

*These can be found in the specialty section at the grocery store or in any Oriental store.

🦃 CLAM CHOWDER 🦃

Not a gourmet recipe, but much better than some restaurants serve.

Makes about 6 main dish servings or 12 first course servings.

- 1/2 cup diced ham or bacon
- 1 medium onion, diced
- 1/4 cup chopped celery
- 2 8-ounce cans minced clams, drained, reserving the liquid
- 2 tablespoons cornstarch
- 4 large potatoes, diced
- 4 cups milk
- 2 tablespoons butter or margarine
- 1 tablespoon salt
- 1/4 teaspoon pepper

In a large saucepan or Dutch oven, cook ham or bacon over medium heat, until lightly browned. Add onions and celery and cook until tender, about 5 minutes. Add enough water to clam liquid to make 2 cups. Mix cornstarch in the clam and water liquid. Add potatoes and clam liquid to the onion and celery mixture, stirring constantly until mixture is slightly thickened. Cover and cook about 10 minutes. Add clams, milk, butter, salt and pepper. Cover and cook until heated through, about 5 minutes more, stirring occasionally.

🌶 MINORCAN CLAM CHOWDER 🌶

This recipe came from the Ford Times Magazine, therefore it must be from a very good restaurant, because that is what they publish.

This is very different from Manhattan or New England clam chowder, but very delicious. The seafood seasoning makes it a little hot, so if you prefer it milder, cut down on the amount used.

Serves 8.

- 2 cups thinly sliced carrots
- 1/2 cup chopped onion
- 2 cups chopped celery
- 1 tablespoon bacon fat
- 3 6-ounce cans minced clams with juice
- 1 teaspoon salt or to taste
- 1/2 teaspoon black pepper
- 2 tablespoons Old Bay seafood seasoning
- 1 tablespoon oregano flakes
- 3 tablespoons fresh chopped parsley
- 2 bay leaves, crushed
- 4 cups whole canned tomatoes, crushed
- 2 cups potatoes, diced

Saute carrots, onions and celery in bacon fat until tender. Add clams with juice, seasonings and tomatoes. Simmer 30 minutes. Add potatoes and simmer until potatoes are tender.

❦ CREAM OF BROCCOLI SOUP ❦

Serves 8 to 10.

- 2 cups thinly sliced onions
- 2 cups thinly sliced leeks*
- 6 tablespoons unsalted butter
- 4 cups thinly sliced broccoli (about 1¾ pounds)
- 4 cups chicken stock or canned chicken broth
- 2 cups heavy cream
- ¾ teaspoon salt
- ¼ teaspoon pepper
- Cayenne pepper to taste

In a large pan, cook onion and leeks in butter over medium heat for 10 minutes or until softened. Add broccoli and chicken stock. Bring to boil, then cover and simmer for 10 minutes or until the broccoli is tender. In a food processor fitted with the steel blade or in a blender, puree the mixture in small batches. Add cream, salt, pepper and Cayenne pepper. Place over medium heat until heated through. Ladle the soup into heated bowls.

*Leeks are a pain to clean, but you must be sure you have removed all the sand.

❦ CHILLED ZUCCHINI SOUP ❦

This recipe serves 10 to 12. Originally, I was going to halve the ingredients in this recipe and make it a recipe that would serve 5 to 6 people. Then I realized that you know how to divide.

I highly recommend this soup as a starter for that elegant dinner party you are to have soon.

- 1 leek*
- 1/4 cup butter or margarine
- 1 cup chopped onion
- 1 cup cubed, pared potatoes
- 1 14-ounce can chicken broth
- 1 teaspoon salt
- 6 cups sliced, unpared zucchini (2 pounds)
- 1 cup milk
- 1 teaspoon dried dillweed or 1 tablespoon chopped fresh dill
- 1/8 teaspoon dried tarragon leaves
- Dash white pepper
- 1 cup light cream
- Snipped chives or fresh dill (for garnish)

Trim leek; cut off root end and green stems. Leek should be about 7 inches long after trimming. Cut leek in half lengthwise, then wash thoroughly. Slice leek crosswise, about 1/8 inch thick.

In hot butter in a 5-quart Dutch oven or kettle, saute leek and onion, stirring, over medium heat, until soft but not brown, about 5 minutes. Add potatoes, chicken broth and salt to leek mixture. Bring to boiling; reduce heat and simmer, covered, 20 minutes. Add zucchini, simmer, covered, 10 minutes or until potatoes are soft. Remove from heat.

Put zucchini mixture into a blender or food processor container, 2 cups at a time and blend at low speed until mixture is smooth. Puree should measure about 7 cups.

In a small saucepan, heat milk until bubbles form around the edge of the pan. Remove from heat. Add hot milk to the zucchini puree. Add dillweed, tarragon and pepper; mix well. Stir in cream.

Refrigerate, covered, 6 hours or overnight. To serve, pour into chilled soup cups or bowls; sprinkle with chives or fresh dill.

*Leeks are a pain to clean - but be sure you remove all the sand. You don't want sandy soup!

❦ LIGHT TOMATO-VEGETABLE SOUP ❦

This recipe gives you a choice of straining the soup and having a light broth or pureeing it and having a little more substantial soup. I choose the latter and have never tried it as a broth.

Serves 4.

- 1 tablespoon butter
- 1 large onion, chopped
- 1 small clove garlic, minced
- 1 small carrot, chopped
- 1 celery stalk (with some leaves), chopped
- 1/4 teaspoon each dried thyme, paprika and dried dillweed
- Generous pinch of cumin
- 4 cups (1 quart) chicken broth
- 2 cups canned tomatoes with liquid, chopped
- Salt and pepper to taste
- 1/4 cup chopped green onion tops (garnish)

Melt butter in heavy, large saucepan over medium heat. Add onion, garlic, carrot, celery, thyme, paprika, dillweed and cumin. Cover and cook until vegetables are wilted, about 15 minutes. Reduce heat and add chicken broth and tomatoes. Cover partially and simmer for 1 hour. Add salt and pepper to taste. If a more robust flavor is desired, uncover and boil 15 minutes.

Strain through a fine sieve for broth or puree in blender (or food processor) for a heartier soup. Reheat and garnish with the green onions.

❦ CHICKEN OR TURKEY WITH RICE SOUP ❦

These are instructions - not a recipe per se. Use your chicken or turkey carcass or save the necks and backs from several chickens for this soup. If using necks and backs, bake at 350°F for about 40 minutes, then proceed as for carcass.

      Carcass of roasted chicken or turkey
1 medium onion, diced
1/2 teaspoon salt
1 cup diced carrots
1 cup diced celery
1 tablespoon chicken base*
3/4 cup uncooked rice

Break carcass apart somewhat to fit in a 4-quart Dutch oven. Cover with water; add onion and salt. Simmer until bits of meat on carcass are very tender, about 1½ hours. Skim off any scum that rises to the top.

Remove bones from pot. Let cool until you can handle easily. Pick all bits of meat from bones and return meat to pot. Discard bones. You should have about 3 quarts of liquid in the pot. Add the carrots, celery and chicken base. Simmer for about 10 minutes.

Add 3/4 cup rice (not the 'minute' rice variety) and simmer until the rice is tender. Taste and salt to your own taste.

*Chicken base can be found in the spice counter of your grocery store. Be sure to refrigerate after opening.

❦ FRENCH ONION SOUP ❦

The restaurant in the Famous Barr Department Store in St. Louis is famous for this soup. It can be frozen, before adding the bread and cheese, of course.

Makes about 4 quarts.

- 3 pounds onions, peeled
- 1/2 cup butter
- 3/4 cup all-purpose flour
- 1 1/2 teaspoons black pepper
- 2 tablespoons paprika
- 1 bay leaf
- 3 quarts beef bouillon*
- 1 cup white wine
- Kitchen Bouquet browning sauce
- 2 teaspoons salt
- French bread
- 1/2 pound sliced Swiss cheese

Slice onions 1/8-inch thick. Melt butter in a large soup pot; add onions and saute slowly for 1 1/2 hours (yes, that's correct). Add flour, pepper, paprika and bay leaf. Saute over low heat 10 minutes more. Add bouillon and wine and simmer for 2 hours. Adjust color to a rich brown with browning sauce. Season to taste with salt. Refrigerate overnight (this is not absolutely necessary, but the soup is really much better the next day).

TO SERVE: Heat soup. Fill ovenproof casserole or individual ovenproof soup bowls with 1 cup soup. Top with 1/2 inch or so thick slices of French bread and top with a slice of cheese.

Place under broiler to brown, approximately 5 minutes, at 550°F.

*You may use homemade beef broth, canned beef broth (diluted if concentrated), or make the broth with beef broth granules found in the soup section of your grocery store.

BEEF AND VEAL

Some of these recipes are more involved than others, but none are beyond the skills of the most inexperienced cook. Read the recipe through first and follow the instructions.

🌾 ROAST BRISKET 🌾

Briskets at this point in time are expensive. If you are not having a crowd, you can use a smaller brisket or cook the large size and freeze some for another meal.

Serves 12.

- 6 to 7 pound beef brisket
- Salt and pepper
- 1 large onion, sliced
- 1/4 cup bottled chili sauce
- 1 tablespoon brown sugar
- 1 clove garlic, crushed
- 1 12-ounce can of beer, opened and allowed to go flat
- 2 tablespoons flour
- 1/2 cup water

Preheat oven to 350°F.

Trim fat from brisket. Season with salt and pepper. Place in a 9x12-inch pan or casserole dish. Cover with sliced onions. Combine chili sauce, brown sugar, garlic and beer and pour over meat. Cover with foil and bake for 4 hours. Cool, degrease and slice meat cross grain. Blend flour and water and add to drippings. Cook until thickened. Pour gravy over meat.

Beef and Veal

🦌 BROILED BEEF TENDERLOIN 🦌
With Mushroom Stuffing and Brandied Tomato Gravy

This is a SUPERB dinner party recipe. The directions are lengthy and it does take a little extra effort, but it is well worth it.

Makes 10 servings.

- 1/2 cup butter or margarine
- 3/4 pound mushrooms, finely chopped
- 4 to 6 ounces sliced, cooked ham, diced
- 1/2 cup minced green onions
- 1/4 teaspoon salt
- 1/4 teaspoon pepper
- 3 cups white bread cubes, (six slices)
- 2 tablespoons water
- 2 1 1/2-pound each beef tenderloin roasts (center pieces)
- Brandied Tomato Gravy (recipe follows)
- Watercress sprigs and cherry tomatoes for garnish

Start preparations about 1 1/2 hours before serving.

PREPARE MUSHROOM STUFFING: In a 12-inch skillet over medium heat, melt butter or margarine; add mushrooms, ham, green onions, salt and pepper; cook until vegetables are tender, stirring frequently. Remove skillet from heat. Add bread cubes and water. Toss gently to mix well. Set aside.

PREPARE TENDERLOINS: Make a lengthwise cut, about 1 1/2-inches deep, along the center of each beef tenderloin roast. Into cut section of each tenderloin, spoon half of the mushroom mixture, packing mixture firmly. With string, tie tenderloins securely in several places to hold cut edges of meat together. (You can buy butcher's string at the hardware store or a kitchen supply store.)

Preheat broiler. Place both tenderloins, cut-side up, on rack of broiler pan; broil 15 minutes. If necessary, cover stuffing with foil to prevent it from browning and drying out. Carefully turn tenderloins, cut-side down and broil 15 minutes longer for rare or until desired doneness. DO NOT OVERCOOK.

Meanwhile, prepare Brandied Tomato Gravy. (Recipe follows.)

TO SERVE: Place tenderloins on cutting board; let stand 10 minutes for easier slicing. Remove string; slice meat. Arrange slices on warm, large platter; garnish with watercress and tomato. Serve gravy in gravy bowl.

BRANDIED TOMATO GRAVY:

Drain one 8-ounce can tomatoes; *reserve liquid.* Finely chop tomatoes; set aside.

In 1-quart saucepan over medium heat, melt 4 tablespoons butter or margarine. Stir in 2 tablespoons all-purpose flour until blended; cook 1 minute. Gradually stir in 1 can beef broth (14-ounces), reserved tomato liquid and tomatoes, 1 tablespoon brandy, $\frac{1}{2}$ teaspoon pepper, $\frac{1}{2}$ teaspoon meat extract* and $\frac{1}{4}$ teaspoon salt. Then cook, stirring constantly, until slightly thickened.

*If you cannot find "meat extract", you can substitute Beef Stock Base, which is a granule and is available in the spice section of your grocery store. It must be refrigerated after opening.

ROAST TENDERLOIN

Another good entre to serve your guests. The only way you can ruin tenderloin is to overcook it.

Serves 8.

- 1 5-pound beef tenderloin roast
- Kitchen Bouquet browning sauce
- Garlic powder
- Salt and cracked black pepper
- 1/2 cup water
- 1/2 cup red wine
- Minced parsley
- Sliced mushrooms, a little or a lot, as you like it

Preheat oven to 500°F.

Using your hands, coat roast well with browning sauce. Season with garlic powder, salt and pepper. Allow to stand until roast is at room temperature. Cook in preheated oven for 25 minutes. Remove roast from pan; cover meat lightly with foil. To pan juices add water, wine, parsley and mushrooms. Simmer until mushrooms are tender and serve as a sauce.

Tenderloin will be brown and crusty on the outside, pink and juicy on the inside. If more doneness is desired, return to oven, but watch carefully because at this temperature every minute counts.

❦ POT ROAST WITH VEGETABLES ❦

You can cut this down for the number of people being served. Better still, cook the entire thing, divide and freeze the leftovers.

Serves 10.

- 1 4 to 5-pound rump roast
- 2 tablespoons salad oil
- 2 tablespoons butter
- 1 small onion, sliced
- 1 clove garlic, crushed
- 1 teaspoon dried thyme leaves
- 1 teaspoon marjoram
- 1 bay leaf, crumbled
- 8 whole peppercorns
- 1 teaspoon salt
- 1 can beef broth, undiluted
- 12 small white onions
- 8 carrots, pared and halved
- 1 sprig parsley
- 1/4 cup water
- 3 tablespoons flour

Wipe roast with paper towels. In hot oil and butter, in 5-quart Dutch oven or heavy kettle, over medium heat, brown roast with sliced onions, turning roast until browned on all sides, about 25 minutes. To the drippings add garlic, thyme, marjoram, bay leaf, black pepper and salt. Saute, stirring for 1/2 minute. Add beef broth. Bring to boil, reduce heat to simmer and cook just below the boiling point, covered, for 2 1/2 hours. Turn meat occasionally so that it will cook evenly. Add onions, carrots and parsley and simmer, covered, 30 minutes longer or until vegetables are tender. Transfer meat and vegetables to warm serving platter; keep warm.

Pour 1/4 cup water into measuring cup; add flour and mix with fork until smooth. Stir into liquid in Dutch oven and bring to a boil, stirring constantly. Reduce heat; simmer 3 minutes. Taste and correct seasonings. Serve gravy over meat.

❦ STANDING RIB ROAST ❦
Prime Rib

With this recipe I've taken liberties with Julia Child's instructions.

Serves 10 or thereabouts.

- 1 5-rib prime roast of beef (have your butcher remove bone but tie it back onto roast to cook)
- 2 tablespoons butter
- 2 medium carrots, roughly chopped (you need not peel)
- 2 medium onions, roughly chopped
- 2 cups beef broth (if using canned broth, dilute somewhat)

Preheat oven to 325°F.

Place rack in lower part of oven. Rub cut ends of beef with the butter. Place roast, ribs down, on a rack in large roasting pan. Bake about 2½ hours for rare to medium rare, basting with drippings occasionally. If you use a meat thermometer, follow directions for desired doneness.

About an hour before roast is done; scatter vegetables into pan.

AU JUS:

Remove roast from roasting pan. Let cool about 15 minutes. Pour off accumulated fat, pour in beef broth and swish about to dislodge any coagulated roasting juices. Pour the liquid and roasting vegetables from pan into a saucepan and simmer, mashing vegetables into the liquid. Season carefully to taste and skim off surface fat.

Just before serving, strain into a hot sauce bowl, adding any juices accumulated from waiting roast.

❦ PAUL'S ROAST BEEF ❦

This is not roasted at all as you will see. It really is not a "recipe" but just directions. The results are great. The number of servings depends upon the size of the roast.

> **Rolled roast of beef**
> **Fresh garlic**
> **Salt and pepper**
> **Fat (oil or lard)**
> **Water**
> **Flour**
> **Kitchen Bouquet browning sauce**

One boneless rolled beef roast, such as rump, sirloin or eye of round. It need not be a particularly tender cut. Size to accommodate the number of people being served.

Puncture meat in numerous places and insert slivers of fresh garlic. Salt and pepper to taste.

Brown roast in Dutch oven on all sides, in small amount of fat. Add water to come up 2 or 3 inches in pot and cook over medium to low heat to desired doneness. We like it rare to medium-rare and according to the size of the roast it will take 45 minutes to 1 hour. You will have to check doneness by cutting a deep slit in meat.

Remove meat to oven proof platter and keep warm in 150°F oven.

Mix 3 to 4 tablespoons flour with $1/2$ to $3/4$ cup water. Strain into liquid in pot, whisking briskly. You must determine when gravy has reached desired thickness. Add browning sauce to get a dark rich color. Strain, if necessary, and serve gravy over meat and over hot cooked rice or mashed potatoes.

Beef and Veal

❧ SPECIAL STEAK B-B-Q ❧

This marinade turns chuck into a very special steak.

Makes 6 servings.

- 1 boneless chuck steak, cut 1½-inches thick, (about 2½ pounds)
- 2 large onions, coarsely chopped (2 cups)
- 2 cloves garlic, peeled
- ¾ cup soy sauce
- 2 teaspoons Spice Island brand Italian herbs
- ¼ cup Kitchen Bouquet browning sauce

Trim fat from around edges of steak, then score remaining fat at 1-inch intervals to keep steak from curling. Place in a glass utility dish.

Combine onions, garlic, soy sauce and Italian herbs in container of an electric blender; cover and process at high speed 1 minute or until mixture is very smooth. Stir in browning sauce.

Pour over steak and allow to stand at room temperature at least 2 hours or up to 8 hours. Remove steak from marinade and reserve marinade.

Build a medium-fire or set gas or electric grill to medium-high, following manufacturer's directions.

Grill steak, 5 inches from heat, 8 minutes per side for rare, 12 minutes per side for medium or 15 minutes per side for well done. Brush with the reserved marinade when you turn roast.

❦ BARBECUED POT ROAST ❦

An inexpensive dish, but you must allow at least six hours for meat to marinade. Better still, marinade overnight.

Serves 4 to 6.

- 1 chuck roast (about 2½ pounds)
- ½ cup soy sauce
- ¼ cup firmly packed brown sugar
- 1 tablespoon lemon juice
- ¼ cup bourbon or brandy
- 1 teaspoon Worcestershire sauce

Place meat in a large shallow casserole dish. Combine remaining ingredients and pour over meat. Cover. Refrigerate for at least 6 hours, turning meat once.

Grill meat 5 inches from hot coals for 10 to 12 minutes on each side for rare, spooning marinade over each time it is turned. To serve, slice on the diagonal.

🍃 SPICY BARBECUED SHORT RIBS 🍃

*What can I tell you? No restaurant serves better short ribs!!
This recipe is for 2 servings but can be multiplied as many times as you like to serve as many people as you want.*

Serves 2.

- 1/8 teaspoon dried thyme
- 2 bay leaves
- 1 teaspoon Tabasco sauce
- 1 onion, chopped
- 1 teaspoon salt
- 1 teaspoon pepper
- 2 pounds lean short ribs, cut into serving pieces

In a kettle combine 1 gallon water, thyme, bay leaves, Tabasco, onion, salt and pepper and bring the water to a boil. Add short ribs and simmer for 1 hour or until they are tender.

FOR THE SAUCE:

- 3/4 cup catsup
- 3 tablespoons Worcestershire sauce
- 1/3 cup packed brown sugar
- 1 tablespoon minced onion
- 1/8 teaspoon chili powder
- 1/4 cup light corn syrup
- 3 tablespoons cider vinegar
- 1 to 2 teaspoons black pepper, to taste
- 1 teaspoon Tabasco sauce*

In a saucepan, combine all sauce ingredients, stir until it is smooth. Heat the sauce over moderate heat until it is hot and keep it hot.

TO FINISH:

Drain the short ribs, pat them dry and arrange them 1 inch apart in a shallow baking pan. Brush the short ribs with the sauce and broil them under a PREHEATED broiler about 4 inches from the heat, turning them frequently and basting them frequently with the sauce, until they are browned. Transfer the remaining sauce to a heated sauceboat. Serve the sauce with the short ribs.

*This may be a bit much. Put in a little and taste.

Beef and Veal

❦ BRAZILIAN BARBECUED BEEF ❦

Another inexpensive dish that is excellent. Cook on the grill.

Serves 6 to 8.

- 1 4-pound beef chuck, 2 to 2½-inches thick
- 1 cup catsup
- ½ cup water
- ⅓ cup vinegar
- ¼ cup cooking oil
- 1 tablespoon instant coffee powder
- 1 teaspoon salt
- ½ teaspoon pepper
- 1 teaspoon chili powder
- 1 teaspoon celery seed
- ⅛ teaspoon garlic powder
- 3 to 4 dashes Tabasco sauce

Using a sharp knife, score fat edges of meat. In bowl, combine all ingredients except the meat. Place meat in shallow baking dish. Pour marinade over meat. Cover and refrigerate several hours or overnight, turning roast several times. Remove from marinade, wiping off excess. Reserve marinade.

Cook over medium-hot coals 20 to 25 minutes per side for rare to medium rare. Brush with marinade occasionally during the last 15 minutes. Heat remaining marinade and pass with meat.

To serve, carve meat in thin slices across grain.

❦ SWISS STEAK ❦

This is not the best recipe "style" but for this recipe it is easier to follow than the usual format. Long slow cooking is the secret of tenderness.

Serves 6.

Combine:

- 1 1/2 teaspoons salt
- 1/2 teaspoon pepper
- 1/4 cup flour

Pound this mixture with tenderizer or edge of saucer into both sides of 2 pounds round steak, cut into serving pieces.

Brown steak on both sides in 2 tablespoons oil.

In blender container place:

- 1 16-ounce can tomatoes
- 1 clove garlic, peeled
- 2 medium onions, peeled and quartered
- 1 rib of celery, sliced in 1-inch pieces
- 6 sprigs parsley

Blend until vegetables are chopped. Pour over steak. Add, if you wish, a pinch of oregano or basil.

Cover and cook gently on top of range for 2 hours or until meat is very tender. If sauce thickens too much, thin it with bouillon, water or red wine.

We like this with mashed potatoes.

ROLLED STUFFED STEAK
Rouladen

Excellent and inexpensive.

Serves 6.

- 6 very thin slices boneless beef
- 1/2 cup chopped onions
- 1/2 cup chopped celery
- 1 tablespoon butter or margarine
- 2 cups crushed herbed stuffing mix
- 1 can beef broth, undiluted
- Shortening
- 1 to 2 tablespoons flour
- Wooden toothpicks

Saute onions and celery in butter until soft, then combine with stuffing mix. Mix in enough beef broth to moisten stuffing. Spread stuffing mix on one side of each slice of beef. Roll up jelly-roll style and secure with wooden toothpicks.

Brown rolls in a little shortening in heavy skillet.

Add remaining beef broth with enough water to make one full can to skillet. Cover and cook over low heat until tender. Remove rolls and keep warm. Mix flour with 1/2 cup water, pour through strainer into pan, stirring till smooth. Cook to desired thickness. Serve gravy over beef rolls.

❦ BEEF STROGANOFF ❦

This is an excellent dish!! Serve it over hot buttered noodles.

Serves 4 to 6.

- 2 tablespoons unsalted butter
- 1½ pounds round steak, cut into 3 by ¼-inch strips
- 2 large onions, sliced
- 1 pound small mushrooms, sliced
- 2 cups canned beef broth
- ¼ teaspoon cayenne
- ¼ teaspoon black pepper
- 1 teaspoon ground nutmeg
- ½ teaspoon dried basil, crumbled
- 1¼ teaspoons salt
- 1 tablespoon cornstarch
- ⅔ cup sour cream
- 1½ tablespoons snipped fresh chives or minced parsley

In a large heavy skillet melt the butter over high heat until the foam subsides and in it brown the beef, turning it often. Add the onions and cook the mixture over moderate heat until the onions are softened. Add the mushrooms, broth, cayenne, black pepper, nutmeg, basil and salt and simmer the mixture, uncovered, stirring occasionally, for 45 minutes or until the beef is tender and the liquid is reduced to about ½ cup. Dissolve the cornstarch in ¼ cup water, stir the mixture into the beef mixture and simmer the mixture, stirring for 1 minute.

Remove the skillet from the heat, stir in the sour cream, then transfer the Stroganoff to a heated serving dish. Garnish with the chives or parsley.

❦ MINUTE STEAKS IN PARSLEY BUTTER ❦

Quick, easy, inexpensive and so good. What more could you ask?

Serves 4 to 6.

- 1/2 cup butter, softened
- 1/4 cup finely chopped parsley
- 8 cubed steaks
- Oil for browning steaks

With fork, blend butter and parsley thoroughly. Set aside. Brush skillet with a little oil. Brown steaks on one side about 2 minutes over high heat, turn and brown on the other side about 1 minute. Top immediately with small balls of the parsley-butter mixture. Serve at once.

❦ LONDON BROIL ❦

You'll be surprised at how good this is!!

Serves 2.

Score one U.S. Choice flank steak (about 1 1/2 pounds) on both sides. Place on the broiler rack; brush with bottled steak sauce, such as A-1. Broil 3 to 4 minutes, 3 inches from heat. Turn, brush again with steak sauce; broil 3 to 4 minutes longer or done as you like it. Just remember that flank steak cooked well done will be tough.

Cut cross grain into thin slices.

🐦 BEEF PEPERONATA 🐦

This can be made using veal, but it will cost you.

Serves 4.

BEEF:

    1/2 cup olive oil
    1/4 cup red wine vinegar
    1 tablespoon fresh lemon juice
    3/4 pound flank steak

PEPERONATA:

    1/4 cup olive oil
    1 large red bell pepper, cut julienne
    1 large yellow bell pepper, cut julienne
    1 small onion, thinly sliced
    1 tablespoon capers with juice
    Salt and freshly ground pepper
    1 tablespoon red wine vinegar
    1 1/2 teaspoons Paul Prudhomme's Cajun Magic blackened meat seasoning mix*
    1/4 teaspoon salt
    1/4 teaspoon freshly ground pepper
    1 teaspoon minced fresh parsley

FOR BEEF:

Mix oil, vinegar and lemon juice in small bowl. Place beef in large shallow baking dish. Pour marinade over. Cover with plastic wrap and refrigerate at least 4 hours or overnight. →

FOR PEPERONATA:

Heat oil in heavy large deep skillet over medium-high heat. Add peppers, onion and capers with juices. Season with salt and pepper. Cook until vegetables are just tender, stirring frequently, about 8 minutes. Add vinegar and bring to boil. Remove skillet from heat.

Prepare barbecue (medium-high heat) or preheat broiler. Remove beef from marinade; reserve marinade. Sprinkle Cajun Magic seasoning, ¼ teaspoon salt and ¼ teaspoon pepper over beef. Grill about 4 minutes per side for medium-rare, brushing occasionally with marinade. Transfer to cutting board. Let stand 2 minutes. Cut meat across grain into thin diagonal slices. Fan slices on plates.

Rewarm peperonata over medium heat. Mix in parsley. Spoon peperonata onto plates.

*Can be found in the spice section in your supermarket.

❦ SALISBURY BOURGUIGNONNE ❦

This is a fancy name for ground beef patties served over noodles.

Serves 6.

    1 can mushroom soup, divided
    1 1/2 pounds ground beef
    1/2 cup fine dry bread crumbs
    1 egg, slightly beaten
    1/4 teaspoon salt
    3 slices bacon
    1/3 cup water
    1/4 cup Burgundy wine or other dry red wine
    1 clove garlic, minced
    1/4 teaspoon dried marjoram leaves, crushed
    Hot cooked egg noodles

Mix thoroughly 1/3 cup soup, beef, bread crumbs, egg and salt. Shape into 6 oval patties. In skillet, cook bacon until crisp; remove and crumble. Set aside. Pour off all but 2 tablespoons of drippings. Brown patties in drippings. Stir in remaining soup, water, wine and seasonings. Cover; simmer 20 minutes. Stir occasionally. Serve over cooked noodles. Garnish with bacon.

🐄 BEEF BURGUNDY 🐄

Freeze some for another day.

Serves 6 or more.

- 2 tablespoons vegetable oil
- 1/8 pound salt pork, diced
- 3 carrots, sliced
- 2 pounds beef, cut into cubes
- Salt, pepper and sugar
- 3 onions, chopped
- 1 clove garlic, minced
- 1/2 pound mushrooms, sliced
- 1/2 bottle red burgundy
- 1/2 cup cognac or other brandy

In a 4-quart casserole, heat oil slightly and spread evenly over bottom and sides. Arrange in layers, 1/2 the salt pork, all the carrots and 1/3 of the beef. Sprinkle with salt, pepper and a pinch of sugar. Add in layers, 1/2 the onions, 1/2 the garlic, 1/2 the mushrooms and 1/3 the beef. Sprinkle with salt, pepper and a pinch of sugar.

Add in layers, remaining onions, garlic, mushrooms, salt pork and beef. Sprinkle again with salt, pepper and a pinch of sugar.

Pour wine and cognac over and bring casserole rapidly to a boil; reduce heat and simmer, covered (liquid should barely bubble), for 2 1/2 hours or until meat is tender.

To reduce liquid, remove cover and continue to simmer for a few minutes more.

❦ MEAT LOAF ❦

The sauce is a barbecue flavor and it is excellent.

Serves 6.

- 1 pound ground beef
- 1 cup fresh bread crumbs
- 1 onion, finely chopped
- 1 egg, beaten
- 1 1/2 teaspoons salt
- 1/4 teaspoon pepper
- 2 small cans tomato sauce, divided
- 3 tablespoons vinegar
- 1/2 cup water
- 3 tablespoons brown sugar
- 2 teaspoons Worcestershire sauce
- 2 tablespoons prepared mustard

Preheat oven to 350°F.

Mix beef, crumbs, onion, egg, salt and pepper and 1/2 cup tomato sauce. Form into loaf and place in shallow pan. Combine rest of ingredients and pour over loaf. Bake for 1 hour and 15 minutes. Baste occasionally.

MEAT BALL STROGANOFF

Serves 4.

- 1 pound ground beef
- 1 small onion, chopped fine
- 1/3 cup bread crumbs
- 1/2 teaspoon dried parsley flakes
- 1 egg
- 1/2 cup cold water
- 1/4 teaspoon pepper
- 2 tablespoons beef fat or oil
- 1 1/2 tablespoons flour
- 2 cups beef broth
- 1/4 cup sour cream
- 1 4-ounce can sliced mushrooms, drained
- 3 cups hot buttered noodles

Preheat oven to 375°F.

Combine beef, onion, crumbs, parsley flakes, egg, water and pepper. Form mixture into 1/2-inch meatballs. Bake in a single layer on a *greased* baking pan for 15 minutes to brown. Keep warm.

In a saucepan melt beef fat or oil, add flour and cook over low heat until mixture is light brown. Heat broth and add to browned flour. Whip until smooth. Cook five minutes. Add sour cream and mushrooms. Pour sauce over meatballs. Serve meatballs over hot noodles.

🌶 BURRITOS 🌶

A friend gave me this recipe but I had to make a solemn promise that I would give it to no one. Please don't tell her you have it. We like to have these served along with tacos.

Serves about 6 to 8. (Makes 10 burritos.)

- 1 1/2 to 2 pounds cooked beef or pork*
- 1 28-ounce can tomatoes, crushed
- 1 can green chiles and tomatoes**
- 1 small can green chiles**
- 3 or 4 tablespoons hot taco sauce
- 1 can refried beans
- 1 package flour tortillas
- 1/2 pound longhorn cheese, cubed
- 1/2 pound longhorn cheese, grated

Preheat oven to 375°F.

Cube meat. Add water to cover and simmer until very tender. Add tomatoes, green chiles and tomatoes, green chiles and taco sauce.

Cook down. (In other words, simmer until meat literally falls apart and liquid has mostly evaporated. At this point, I use a potato masher and mash to break up the meat.)

Spread refried beans on tortillas. Cover with meat mixture. Put several cubes of cheese across and roll up. Place seam side down in baking dish. Sprinkle grated cheese on top. Bake until cheese is melted. Serve with additional taco sauce.

*Use your leftover meat. You can mix pork and beef for this recipe.

**You will find the green chiles and tomatoes and the green chiles in the specialty section of your grocery store along with the taco sauce.

🦌 BAKED LASAGNA 🦌

I found this recipe on a box of lasagna noodles years ago and it is still the favorite of my family. It makes one quite large casserole or you can divide it into 2 smaller casserole dishes and freeze one before it is cooked. This is one of the exceptions where the pasta does freeze well.

Serves 8 to 10.

- 1 pound ground beef
- 1 tablespoon olive oil
- 1 medium onion, chopped
- 1 clove garlic, minced
- 1 teaspoon chopped parsley
- 2 6-ounce cans tomato paste
- 1 teaspoon Italian spices*
- 2 cups water
- 1/2 teaspoon salt
- 1/2 teaspoon pepper
- 1 pound lasagna noodles
- 2 eggs
- 3/4 pound cottage or ricotta cheese
- 3/4 pound mozzarella cheese, sliced
- Grated Parmesan cheese

Preheat oven to 375°F.

Brown beef in olive oil with onion, garlic and parsley. Add tomato paste, Italian spices, two cups water, salt and pepper and simmer 1½ hours.

Add lasagna noodles to 6 quarts of salted boiling water, stirring almost constantly to prevent sticking together and cook 15 minutes or until tender. Drain.

Mix eggs and ricotta. Arrange lasagna in baking dish in layers, alternating with layers of sauce, mozzarella and ricotta-egg mixture until lasagna is all used. Save a little sauce to spread on top. Sprinkle with Parmesan cheese. Bake about 20 minutes.

*You can find Italian spices in the spice rack at the grocery store. It is a ready mixed blend of several spices.

❧ VEAL CORDON BLEU ❧

My family does not like veal enough to justify the price it commands, so I don't use it often. This is so good that I'm including it.

Serves 6.

- 1½ pounds veal, sliced and pounded thin
- 6 thin slices baked ham
- 6 slices Swiss cheese
- ¼ cup all-purpose flour
- ¼ teaspoon salt
- 2 eggs, beaten
- ½ cup milk
- 1½ cups bread crumbs
- 6 tablespoons butter
- Lemon slices and parsley for garnish

Preheat oven to 350°F.

Cut veal into 6 serving size pieces; top each slice of veal with ham and cheese. Fold in half or roll up and pin with wooden toothpicks. In one dish, combine flour and salt. In second dish, combine eggs and milk. Put bread crumbs in a third dish. Coat veal lightly in flour mixture, then in egg-milk mixture, then into bread crumbs. Melt butter in large skillet; fry over medium heat until golden brown. Finish in oven for about 25 minutes. Garnish with lemon slices and parsley.

❦ BRAISED VEAL SHANKS ❦

This is one of the best recipes I've ever found. In gourmet circles it is called Boco Osso. With a salad and mashed potatoes it is an elegant meal.

Makes 4 servings.

- 1/4 cup all-purpose flour
- Salt and pepper
- 4 (2-inch thick) veal shanks
- 2 tablespoons butter, divided
- 1 tablespoon olive oil
- 4 garlic cloves
- 1 cup dry white wine
- 2 cups canned chicken broth
- 2 tablespoons Italian herb seasoning
- 1 tablespoon lemon juice
- 2 1/2 teaspoons grated lemon peel
- 2 tablespoons all-purpose flour

Preheat oven to 350°F.

Season 1/4 cup flour with salt and pepper. Dredge veal shanks in flour; shake off excess. Melt 1 tablespoon butter with oil in heavy large skillet over medium heat. Add garlic and saute until browned, about 5 minutes. Remove garlic and discard. Increase heat to medium-high. Add veal shanks to same skillet and cook until browned, about 4 minutes per side. Place veal shanks in a metal 8 1/2 x 11-inch baking pan.

Increase heat to high. Add wine to skillet and bring to boil, scraping up any browned bits. Pour over veal. Add broth to baking pan. Sprinkle herb seasoning, lemon juice and peel over. Cover and bake until veal is tender, turning once, about 1 1/2 hours. →

Transfer veal shanks to platter; keep warm. Degrease pan juices. Mix remaining 1 tablespoon of butter with flour to form paste; whisk into juices. Simmer until reduced to 1 cup. Pour gravy over veal shanks. Serve hot.

🌶 PEPPER STEAK 🌶

You could classify this as an Oriental dish, but only because it contains soy sauce. Wherever you want to file it, it is an excellent dish.

Serves 4.

- 1 pound round steak
- 2 tablespoons vegetable oil
- 3 large tomatoes, cut into wedges
- 2 medium green peppers, cut into 1-inch cubes
- 2 tablespoons soy sauce
- 1/4 teaspoon sugar
- 1/4 teaspoon garlic salt
- 2 medium onions, sliced
- 1/4 teaspoon pepper
- 1/8 teaspoon ground ginger
- 3/4 cup beef broth plus 1/4 cup beef broth
- 1 tablespoon cornstarch

Partially freeze steak; slice across grain into 2x1/4-inch strips.

Heat oil in large skillet. Cook steak in oil until lightly browned. Stir in tomatoes, green peppers, soy sauce, sugar, garlic salt, onions, pepper, ginger and 3/4 cup beef broth. Simmer for about 15 minutes.

Combine cornstarch with 1/4 cup beef broth and stir into steak mixture. Simmer until slightly thickened.

Can be cooked longer if you want the vegetables more tender.

❧ "HOT" STIR FRIED BEEF ❧

Serves 4.

- 1   1½-pound beef flank steak or top round steak
- 1   bunch green onions, cut into 3-inch pieces
- 3   tablespoons soy sauce
- 3   tablespoons catsup
- 2   tablespoons dry sherry or dry vermouth
- 1   tablespoon cornstarch
- 1   tablespoon peeled and minced ginger root or 1 teaspoon ground ginger
- ½   teaspoon ground red pepper
- 4   medium carrots
- 4   medium celery stalks
-     Vegetable oil
- ½   teaspoon salt

ABOUT ONE HOUR BEFORE SERVING: Cut steak into thin slices, about ⅛-inch thick and 2 or 3 inches in length. In medium bowl, mix meat strips, green onions, soy sauce, catsup, sherry, cornstarch, ginger and ground red pepper; set aside. With knife, cut carrots and celery into 3-inch-long matchstick-thin strips.

In a wok or 10-inch skillet over medium to high heat, in 3 tablespoons hot vegetable oil, cook carrots, celery and salt, stirring quickly and frequently (stir-frying) until vegetables are tender-crisp, about 3 minutes. Spoon vegetables into medium bowl.

In same wok or skillet over high heat, in ¼ cup more hot salad oil, stir-fry meat mixture about 3 minutes or until meat loses its pink color and is tender, stirring frequently. Remove wok or skillet from heat; stir in vegetables. Spoon meat mixture onto a warm large platter. Serve with hot, cooked rice.

❦ STIR-FRIED BEEF WITH STRING BEANS ❦

Very, very good. Again, don't be put off by the list of ingredients or length of directions. With any Chinese dish you should do all the chopping and mixing ahead of time and have it nearby, ready to use as it is called for in the recipe. The cooking time for Chinese food is minimal, but preparing the ingredients can take awhile.

Serves 4 to 6.

- 1 teaspoon sugar
- 1 tablespoon cornstarch
- 1 teaspoon Ac'cent
- 2 tablespoons soy sauce
- 1/2 cup chicken broth
- 1/4 cup vegetable oil, divided
- 1/8 teaspoon salt
- 2 slices ginger root, cut into thin strips
- 1 clove garlic, minced
- 1 1/2 to 2 cups sliced lean beef (about 1 pound, boneless)
- 1 pound string beans, ends and strings removed and beans broken in half
- 6 dried Chinese mushrooms, presoaked in 1 cup water, stems removed and discarded and mushrooms cut into thin strips
- 1 cup bamboo shoots, cut into thin strips
- 4 green onions, cut into 1 1/2 lengths, including green tops
- 2 tablespoons sherry
- Sprigs of Chinese parsley (garnish)

Mix together first five ingredients and set aside. Heat wok or pan hot and dry. Add half of the vegetable oil. Add the salt. Turn heat to medium and add the ginger and garlic to fry until golden brown. →

Turn up heat to high and add the sliced beef, stirring constantly until the outside has browned. Shut off the heat, remove beef from pan and set aside.

Heat wok or pan again and the remainder of the oil.

Add the string beans, mushrooms, bamboo shoots and green onions and fry for 2 minutes while stirring. Check for doneness by observing color of the beans. When they've turned a deep bright green, they're done.

Add the sherry and cover quickly to cook 1 minute longer. Put back the beef. Stir well and add the sauce mixture from group 3. Cook until gravy thickens. Put in serving dish and top with Chinese parsley. Serve with hot cooked rice.

❦ GRILLED REUBEN SANDWICHES ❦
Double Deckers

Serves 6.

    1 cup commercial Thousand Island dressing
  18 slices rye bread
  12 slices Swiss cheese
  ½ cup canned sauerkraut
  24 slices thinly-sliced corned beef
      Butter or margarine, softened

Spread Thousand Island dressing on one side of 12 slices of bread. Arrange 1 slice of cheese, 2 teaspoons sauerkraut and 2 slices of corned beef evenly over each slice of bread. Stack to make 6 (2-layer) sandwiches; top with remaining bread.

Spread butter on outside of top slice of bread; invert sandwiches onto a hot skillet or griddle. Cook until bread is golden. Spread butter on ungrilled side of bread; carefully turn sandwiches and cook until bread is golden and cheese is slightly melted. Secure sandwiches with wooden toothpicks. Cut crosswise into 3 pieces. Serve hot.

PORK

Pork has lost some of its popularity in recent years. At one time it was the mainstay of all farmers. They made smoked sausages, hams and other things and salt cured other cuts. They had no freezers!! Now we have excellent fresh, smoked, cured and any other kind of pork you would want. There are lots of excellent ways to prepare it. Try some of these recipes.

❦ BUTTERFLIED LOIN OF PORK ❦

This is a Julia Child recipe (with some slight modifications) that is a great, economical company dish. It is no trouble at all to make.

Serves 6 to 8 with leftovers.

- 1   7-pound pork loin (bone removed)
- 2 or 3 large garlic cloves
- 2 teaspoons salt
- 1/2 teaspoon each dried rosemary and thyme
- 1/8 teaspoon powdered allspice
-   About 3 tablespoons olive oil
- 1 or more teaspoons Kosher or sea salt

Preheat oven to 375°F.

Have butcher remove the bone (butterflying) from the pork loin. Puree garlic cloves and 2 teaspoons salt. Crumble rosemary. Add rosemary, thyme and allspice to pureed garlic, then stir in oil. (You can put the garlic through a garlic press, crumble the rosemary by hand and mix with salt, thyme, allspice and oil.) Spread the flesh side of the pork with this marinade. Refrigerate and marinate for at least 2 hours.

Roast the pork, basting with accumulated juices in pan, for about an hour. Remove roast to another roasting pan. Preheat broiler to very hot. Score roast on fat side. Sprinkle with a thin layer of coarse salt. Place meat 3 inches from heat and let it brown.

Skim off fat from roasting juices and spoon a little of the juices over the meat. Pour the rest into a hot sauce bowl and moisten each serving with a spoonful.

🦌 GERMAN-STYLE PORK SCHNITZEL 🦌

When my husband returned from a business trip to Germany, he asked me to make Schnitzel. After a lengthy search, I found this recipe which he loves.

Serves 6.

- 6 boneless pork loin cutlets (about 2 pounds total), trimmed
- 1/2 cup all-purpose flour
- 2 teaspoons seasoned salt
- 1/2 teaspoon freshly ground pepper
- 2 eggs
- 1/4 cup milk
- 1 1/2 cup fresh bread crumbs
- 1/2 teaspoon paprika
- 6 tablespoons Crisco shortening, divided
- 2 tablespoons all-purpose flour
- 1/2 teaspoon dried dillweed
- 1 1/2 cup chicken broth
- 1 cup sour cream, at room temperature

Place cutlets between 2 sheets of waxed paper and flatten to 1/4 to 1/2-inch thickness. Cut small slits around edges of pork to prevent curling. Set aside.

Combine 1/2 cup flour, salt and pepper in shallow bowl or on a sheet of waxed paper. Beat eggs with milk in another shallow bowl.

Mix crumbs and paprika in small bowl or on another sheet of waxed paper. Melt 3 tablespoons Crisco in large skillet over medium heat. Dip cutlets in flour, then into egg mixture. Coat with crumbs, covering completely. Add 3 cutlets to skillet and saute on both sides, until coating is golden brown and meat is no longer pink, about 3 to 5 minutes per side. Transfer to platter and keep warm. Repeat with remaining shortening and cutlets.

Combine remaining flour with dillweed. Add to skillet, scraping up any browned bits clinging to the bottom of the pan. Add broth, stirring constantly, until well blended. Stir in sour cream and cook until heated through. DO NOT BOIL. Spoon over cutlets or pass separately.

🦌 APPLE GLAZED PORK ROAST 🦌

This is a beautifully glazed, browned pork roast. Do not overcook. That is the greatest sin you can commit against pork. Now it is known that to cook pork to 165 degrees internally is more than enough. You can even have a little pink and not fret.

Serves 6.

- 1 12-ounce jar apple jelly
- 4 teaspoons Dijon mustard
- 3 teaspoons lemon juice, divided
  Salt and pepper
- 1 boned and tied pork loin, rib-end roast (2½ pounds), at room temperature
- 1 tablespoon brandy

Preheat oven to 350°F.

In small saucepan, melt jelly over low heat. Stir in mustard and 1 teaspoon lemon juice; set aside. Rub roast generously with salt and pepper. Place on rack in shallow foil-lined roasting pan. Roast for 45 minutes. Brush lightly with jelly mixture and continue roasting, brushing with jelly once more, 30 to 45 minutes. Let stand at room temperature for about 10 minutes.

Scrape any browned drippings from roasting pan into remaining jelly. Add remaining 2 teaspoons lemon juice and the brandy. Heat through and season with salt and pepper. Slice roast thin. Pass sauce with roast.

🍎 ROAST PORK WITH SWEET POTATOES AND APPLES 🍎

This is a good Southern-style roast.

Serves 8 to 10.

- 1 5-pound pork loin roast, with the backbone sawed through, but attached and tied to the loin with a cord (your butcher will know what I mean).
- 1 teaspoon salt
- 1/2 teaspoon black pepper
- 3 sweet potatoes, peeled and cut in half lengthwise
- 6 tart, firm red apples, cored
- 1 teaspoon cinnamon, mixed with 1/4 cup brown sugar

Preheat oven to 350°F.

Rub the pork loin with the salt and pepper and place it fat side up in a large roasting pan. For the most predictable results, use a meat thermometer. Roast loin for 45 minutes, then place the sweet potatoes around it and roast for another 15 minutes. Fill the hollows of the apples with the sugar-cinnamon mixture, dividing it evenly among them and stand the apples upright in the pan. Continue to roast for 30 minutes or until the meat thermometer registers 165°F. Transfer the roast to a heated platter and let it stand for about 10 minutes for easier slicing. Surround the roast with the sweet potatoes and apples.

Skim and discard the fat from the juices in the roasting pan and serve the gravy in a gravy boat.

❧ COUNTRY-STYLE SPARERIBS AND POTATOES IN BASIL TOMATO SAUCE ❧

This recipe came from a gourmet magazine. For years they printed their recipes with the ingredients listed as you came to them in the recipe. I always find that type of recipe hard to follow and also I dislike having to read the recipe through just in order to list the ingredients for my shopping list. I have listed the ingredients at the top of the recipe and hope it is helpful to you.

Serves 6.

- 1 cup dry white wine
- 1 6-ounce can tomato paste
- 1/4 cup minced fresh basil or 1 tablespoon dried*
- 3 large garlic cloves, mashed
- 1 teaspoon each salt and pepper
- 1/4 teaspoon ground allspice
- 3 pounds country-style spareribs
- 1 1/2 pounds boiling potatoes, peeled and quartered
- 1 1/2 cups beef broth
- 1 teaspoon salt
- 1/2 cup beef broth
- Minced parsley

Preheat oven to 450°F.

In a large ceramic or glass bowl combine wine, tomato paste, basil, garlic cloves, salt and pepper and allspice. Add spareribs, turning to coat them with marinade and let them marinate, covered and chilled, for 6 hours or overnight.

Let the spareribs and the marinade come to room temperature, transfer the ribs with tongs to a shallow baking pan, large enough to hold them in one layer. Pour the marinade into a stainless steel or enameled saucepan. Add to the saucepan the potatoes, 1½ cups beef broth and 1 teaspoon salt. Bring the liquid to a boil and simmer the potatoes, covered, for 20 to 25 minutes or until they are tender.

Transfer the potatoes with a slotted spoon to a plate and keep them warm and covered. Reduce the cooking liquid over moderately high heat to about ¾ cup and keep the sauce warm.

Meanwhile bake the ribs in the upper third of the oven, turning them once, for 30 minutes or until they are well browned and tender. Transfer them to a heated platter and pour off the fat in the pan. Add ½ cup beef broth to the baking pan and deglaze the pan by scraping up the brown bits clinging to the bottom and stirring the broth into the sauce. Arrange the potatoes around the ribs, sprinkle them with the minced parsley and pour the sauce over the ribs.

*This recipe originally called for thyme, but I once used basil by mistake and we liked it much better. You can take your choice.

❦ CHINESE PORK ROAST OR SPARERIBS ❦

Serves 4.

MARINADE:

    4 tablespoons soy sauce
    1/8 teaspoon 5-spice powder*
    1 tablespoon wine
    3 teaspoons water
    3 tablespoons Hoisin sauce*
    3 or 4 teaspoons sugar
    1/2 teaspoon salt

Mix all ingredients together. Set aside.

    2 pounds or so boneless pork butt
    2 teaspoons Hoisin sauce*
    Red food coloring
    Water

Preheat oven to 350°F.

Cut pork into large strips (about 4 inches long, 1½ inches thick and 1½ inches wide). Score with diagonal cuts ¼-inch deep at 1½-inch intervals on two opposite sides. Marinate pork in a shallow dish for three hours at room temperature or overnight in the refrigerator. Turn meat occasionally. Remove pork. Add a few drops of red food coloring, 2 teaspoons Hoisin sauce and enough water to the marinade to make about ¼ cup of sauce.

Put 1 cup water in bottom of broiler pan. Place meat on broiler rack and bake for 30 minutes. Turn meat and bake another 30 minutes. Turn heat up to 400°F. Brush sauce on meat and bake 3 to 5 minutes longer. Turn meat, brush again with sauce and bake 3 to 5 minutes longer.

For spareribs use 3 pounds of spareribs and follow the same procedure as above.

*5-spice powder and Hoisin sauce can be found in the Chinese section of your grocery store or in an Oriental market.

🌺 CHINESE-HAWAIIAN BARBECUED RIBS 🌺

This is not only a great entree, but is excellent as appetizers if you use baby spareribs.

Serves 3 or 4.

- 1 tablespoon grated fresh ginger root
- 1/2 clove garlic, put through a garlic press
- 1/2 cup soy sauce
- 3/4 cup sugar
- 1/2 cup catsup
- 4 tablespoons sherry
- 1 teaspoon salt
- 1 large slab of pork loin ribs

Preheat oven to 325°F.

Place all ingredients, except ribs, in a bowl. Mix well. Rub mixture into slab of ribs. Marinate for 3 hours. Place ribs on rack and put a little water in the bottom of the broiler pan. Bake ribs on rack for 45 minutes, turning once. Baste during cooking time with remaining marinade. Turn ribs once during cooking time.

Remove ribs from rack, cut apart, then serve hot.

❦ BRANDIED PORK STEAK ❦
For the Grill

Apple brandy, mustard and pumpkin pie spice make pork elegant eating. Let the steak marinate for at least 1 hour.

Serves 4.

- 1 center-cut pork steak, cut 1-inch thick (about 1 1/2 pounds)
- 1/3 cup apple brandy
- 1/2 cup firmly packed brown sugar
- 2 tablespoons prepared sharp mustard
- 1 teaspoon pumpkin pie spice

Trim excess fat from steak; score remaining fat at 1-inch intervals.

Pour brandy over pork steak in a glass dish and allow to stand at room temperature for 1 hour. Remove steak and reserve brandy.

Build a medium fire or set electric or gas grill to medium, following manufacturer's instructions. Grill, turning once, 15 minutes.

While steak grills, combine reserved brandy, brown sugar, mustard and pumpkin pie spice in a small metal saucepan with a flameproof handle. Heat on the grill, stirring several times, until bubbly-hot.

Baste steak with brown sugar mixture. Grill 5 minutes, turn and baste again and grill 5 minutes longer or until well glazed.

Serve with baked sweet potatoes, if you wish.

🦌 PORK STEAKS, CHINESE STYLE 🦌

As with any Chinese dish, this is served with rice. You can use pork chops, if you prefer.

Serves 4.

- 1 clove garlic, minced
- 3 green onions, chopped
- 1 teaspoon sugar
- 1/2 teaspoon Ac'cent
- 1/3 cup soy sauce
- 2 tablespoons sherry
- A dash of Tabasco sauce
- 4 pork steaks
- 2 tablespoons vegetable oil

Combine garlic, green onions, sugar, Ac'cent, soy sauce, sherry and Tabasco to make marinade. Trim most of the fat from steaks. Place steaks in a shallow dish. Pour marinade over, turning several times to coat all surfaces. Let stand for 2 hours or more. Remove steaks from marinade (reserve marinade). Dry steaks with paper towels.

Heat oil in heavy skillet. Brown steaks in skillet about 7 to 10 minutes per side. Pour marinade over steaks, cover and cook 1 minute more. Remove steaks to serving plates, pour gravy over and serve.

You can marinade the steaks overnight if it is more convenient.

🌶 HUNGARIAN PORK PAPRIKA 🌶

Serves 4.

- 2 tablespoons flour
- 1 tablespoon paprika
- 1/2 teaspoon salt
- 1/4 teaspoon pepper
- 1 pound boneless lean pork, cut into 1-inch cubes
- 4 teaspoons olive oil
- 2 14-ounce cans stewed tomatoes
- 1/2 cup sour cream, room temperature

Combine flour, paprika, salt and pepper. Toss with meat. In skillet, brown meat in hot oil. Stir in tomatoes. Cook, uncovered, over medium heat 20 minutes or until meat is tender, stirring frequently. Remove pan from heat. Remove 1/2 cup of sauce mixture from skillet and blend with sour cream. Return mixture to skillet; blend well. DO NOT BOIL. Serve over hot noodles.

❧ BROILED MUSTARD PORK CHOPS ❧

Makes 4 servings.

- 1 large garlic clove, finely minced or put through a garlic press
- 2 tablespoons course-grain mustard
- 1/4 cup cider vinegar
- 1/4 cup olive oil
- 1 teaspoon dried rosemary
- 4 center-cut loin pork chops, 1 1/2 inches thick
- Freshly ground pepper

In a medium bowl, whisk together the garlic, mustard and vinegar. Whisk in the olive oil in a slow, thin stream. Stir in the marjoram.

Coat the chops on both sides with the marinade, then marinate for at least 20 to 30 minutes or overnight at room temperature.

Preheat the broiler. Place the chops in the broiler pan and top with any mustard marinade left in the bowl; distribute it evenly over the chops. Sprinkle with pepper to taste. Broil the chops 3 inches from the heat, about 10 minutes on each side, until firm to the touch and cooked through. Serve hot.

❧ SIZZLIN' PORK CHOPS ❧

The key to crusty, tender chops is preheating the pan and oil just until the oil begins to smoke. Cook the chops four minutes per side - no more, honest!

We like brown rice with this.

Serves 8.

- 4 teaspoons Paul Prudhomme's Cajun Magic Pork and Veal Magic Seasoning Mix
- 8 center-cut pork chops (6 ounces each)
- 2 tablespoons vegetable oil, divided
- 1/4 cup all-purpose flour
- 6 tablespoons butter or margarine
- 2 teaspoons minced garlic
- 3 tablespoons chopped parsley
- 2 tablespoon finely chopped green onions

Sprinkle 1/4 teaspoon of Seasoning Mix evenly on each side of each chop and press lightly. Let stand 15 to 30 minutes.

Heat 1 tablespoon oil in large heavy skillet over high heat until just smoking, about 3 minutes. Meanwhile, dredge 4 chops with flour and shake off excess. Add to skillet and cook 4 minutes. Reduce heat to medium-high; turn chops over and cook until dark brown and crisp on outside, about 4 minutes more. Remove from skillet and keep warm. Repeat with remaining oil, flour and chops.

Add butter to skillet and whisk until butter stops sizzling. Add garlic, parsley and green onions; heat about 30 seconds, stirring constantly. Spoon sauce over chops and serve with hot cooked rice.

❧ OLD-TIME PORK TURNOVERS ❧

These are delicious as a hearty snack or as an entree.

Makes 16 turnovers.

- 1½ pounds lean ground pork
- 2 large carrots, peeled and coarsely grated, about 1½ cups
- 4 to 6 scallions, sliced, (about ⅔ cup)
- 1 teaspoon dried sage leaves
- 1 cup coarsely grated mozzarella cheese
- 1 teaspoon salt
- 2 packages frozen puff pastry sheets (4 sheets) thawed
- 1 large egg

PREPARE FILLING:

In 12-inch skillet over medium-high heat, cook pork 5 to 7 minutes, stirring frequently until well browned. Stir in carrots, scallions and sage; cook 5 minutes more. Remove from heat; cool, then stir in cheese and salt. Set aside.

Preheat oven to 425°F.

PREPARE CRUST:

On a lightly floured surface roll each sheet of pastry out to 10-inch square; cut each sheet into four 5-inch squares. Spoon one-sixteenth of pork mixture into center of each square. In small bowl beat egg and 1 tablespoon water. Brush edges of squares lightly with egg mixture; fold each in half to make triangle. Press edges with tines of fork to seal. Brush pastry triangles with egg mixture; bake 15 minutes until puffed and golden.

May be frozen.

❦ HAM AND CHEESE SANDWICHES ❦

These are delicious, can be made ahead, frozen, thawed and baked. Nice to have on hand for those friends who drop in to watch the football game. Yes, you do use both butter and margarine.

- 1 pound shredded ham (or thinly sliced)
- 1/2 pound shredded Swiss cheese (or thinly sliced)
- 16 hamburger buns

SPREAD:

- 1 stick butter, softened
- 1 stick margarine, softened
- 3 tablespoons prepared mustard
- 1 1/2 tablespoons poppy seeds
- 1 teaspoon Worcestershire sauce
- 1 medium onion, grated

Preheat oven to 325°F.

Mix all spread ingredients together. Spread buns with spread mixture. Put on ham and cheese. Wrap individually in foil and bake for 30 minutes.

🍇 HAM FRIED RICE 🍇

Credit for this recipe goes to my sister-in-law who is Chinese. A good way to use up leftover rice and ham. You can also use leftover pork or chicken instead of ham.

The recipe calls for mixing well, but do it gently so that the rice does not become mushy.

- 2 teaspoons shortening or oil
- 5 eggs
- 3/4 to 1 cup diced, cooked ham
- 3 to 4 cups cooked rice (cold)
- 1/2 cup chopped green onions
- 3 tablespoons soy sauce or to taste
- 1 tablespoon Kitchen Bouquet browning sauce

In a large skillet or Dutch oven (preferably non-stick finish), heat shortening; break eggs into heated shortening and scramble. Cook until set. Stir in ham and heat through. Add rice and mix well. Again heat through.

Add onions, then sprinkle with soy sauce over all, stirring well. Taste as you add the soy sauce - you may want more or less. Stir in the browning sauce. Heat through. Serve hot. Do not overcook - onions should be crispy tender.

❦ SLICED HAM WITH ASPARAGUS SPEARS AND EGG SAUCE ❦

This is great to serve to your bridge luncheon group. Use leftover spiral cut ham such as Honey Baked if you have it.

Serves 6.

- 6 tablespoons butter
- 6 tablespoons flour
- 2 cups milk
- Salt and pepper to taste
- 1/4 cup Parmesan cheese
- 3 hard-boiled eggs, sliced
- 6 slices baked ham
- 12 toasted English muffins halves
- 30 asparagus spears, trimmed and cooked

Melt the butter in a saucepan, add the flour and stir with a wire whisk until blended. Meanwhile, bring the milk to a boil and add all at once to the butter-flour mixture, stirring vigorously with the whisk. When thickened, reduce heat and simmer one minute. Season to taste with salt and pepper. Turn off the heat and add the cheese, stirring until smooth. Gently stir in the egg slices to complete the sauce.

Saute the ham slices in a little butter until heated through. Place on toasted English muffin halves. Top each slice with five asparagus spears.

Spoon the egg sauce over the asparagus and serve.

❧ CREAMED HAM AND ARTICHOKES CASSEROLE ❧

This is excellent for a "ladies' luncheon" and it is also good for dinner. It lets you use up leftover ham.

Makes 8 servings.

- 2 9-ounce packages frozen artichoke hearts
- 1 bay leaf (optional)
- 2 cans cream of mushroom soup (undiluted)
- 1 tablespoon chopped onion
- 1/4 cup sherry (or dry vermouth)
- 1/2 teaspoon salt
- 1/4 teaspoon garlic salt
- Pepper
- 2 cups diced, cooked ham
- 8 hard-boiled eggs, quartered
- 4 slices American cheese

Preheat oven to 400°F.

Cook artichoke hearts as directed on package, adding bay leaf during cooking, if desired. Drain; remove bay leaf. Combine soup, onion, sherry, salt, garlic salt and pepper. Mix well. Arrange artichoke hearts, ham and hard-boiled eggs in a 3-quart casserole. Add soup mixture. Top with slices of cheese. Bake for 25 to 30 minutes or until cheese is lightly browned.

POULTRY

This is the most versatile of meats. It can also be a boon to your diet. If you remove the skin and fat before cooking you can reduce calories and cholesterol.

❦ SOUTHERN FRIED CHICKEN ❦

Being a Southerner, I can tell you that there are many ways to make Southern fried chicken and each cook will tell you that their way is the right way. This recipe is good. You can use whole milk, buttermilk or no milk at all instead of evaporated. You can soak the chicken in whole milk, dip it in flour, then in beaten eggs, then in fresh bread crumbs. Lard is much better for taste for frying chicken, but you can use oil or shortening. A well-seasoned iron skillet is preferred but not essential.

Serves 3 to 4.

- 1 cup flour
- 1 teaspoon salt
- 1 teaspoon pepper
- 1 cup evaporated milk
- 1 frying chicken ($2^1/_2$ to 3 pounds), cut up
- 1 to $1^1/_2$ cups lard, oil or shortening

Combine dry ingredients. Dip chicken in milk. Coat with flour mixture. Fry in hot lard until chicken is golden brown and crisp, about ten minutes per side. Check for doneness by piercing a large piece of chicken (breast or thigh). If the juices run clear and there is no pink, the chicken is done.

🌶 GOLDEN CRUNCH FRIED CHICKEN 🌶

This is another good Southern fried chicken recipe. Removing the skin cuts out lots of fat and cholesterol. This batter is also excellent on fish.

Serves 3 to 4.

- 1 2½-pound chicken, cut up
- 1 cup all-purpose flour
- 2 teaspoons salt
- ½ teaspoon pepper
- 1 cup buttermilk
- ½ teaspoon soda
- Fat for frying (lard, shortening or vegetable oil)

Combine flour, salt and pepper in a paper bag, then add one piece of chicken at a time; shake until well coated. Combine the buttermilk and soda in a bowl, then dip the chicken in the buttermilk and shake in the flour mixture again. Fry in about 1½ inches of hot fat for about 10 minutes per side. Drain on paper toweling.

❦ HERB GRILLED CHICKEN ❦

The sauce for this is best made a few hours in advance of using. If refrigerated, whip it for a few seconds before using.

Serves 6.

- 1 cup vegetable oil
- 1 egg
- 1/4 teaspoon pepper
- 1/4 teaspoon oregano
- Pinch of garlic powder
- 1/4 cup cider vinegar
- 1 tablespoon salt
- 1 teaspoon poultry seasoning
- 1/8 teaspoon thyme, crumbled
- Pinch of paprika
- 6 broiler-fryer chicken portions

Combine all ingredients except chicken, in a small bowl. Beat with a fork to blend. Brush over chicken. Grill chicken, skin side up, 6 inches from hot coals, 15 minutes. Turn and baste with sauce. Continue turning and basting about 30 minutes longer or until chicken is tender but not dry.

FOR WHOLE CHICKEN: Adjust and secure chicken on barbecue spit so it will turn freely. Brush all over with sauce. Place spit about 6 inches from hot coals. Start spit rotating and roast chicken, brushing frequently with sauce, about 1 1/2 hours or until juices run clear when thigh area is pierced with fork.

❦ COUNTRY CAPTAIN ❦

This is an elegant dish that you'll want to show off to your guests. You do not have to tell them how simple it is to make.

Serves 10.

- 1 teaspoon each of salt and garlic salt
- 1/2 teaspoon white pepper
- 10 chicken breast halves
- 1 cup all-purpose flour, in a brown paper bag
- Oil for browning chicken
- 2 onions, finely chopped
- 1 1/2 green peppers, chopped
- 1 garlic clove, chopped
- 2 teaspoons curry powder
- 2 16-ounce cans tomatoes, chopped
- 1 teaspoon chopped parsley
- 6 large tablespoons currents
- 1 teaspoon thyme
- 1/4 pounds blanched almonds
- Hot cooked rice

Preheat oven to 325°F.

Salt and pepper the chicken breasts, using the salt, garlic salt and white pepper. Shake chicken in flour and brown quickly in oil. Remove chicken and place in large casserole (9x13).

Saute onion, green pepper and garlic in a little oil. Add remaining ingredients except almonds. Pour over chicken, cover with foil and bake for 45 minutes.

Toast almonds on a cookie sheet until slightly brown. Sprinkle almonds over casserole and serve with hot cooked rice.

You can divide this recipe or freeze half of the recipe before you add the almonds.

🐦 CHICKEN HEKKA 🐦

This came from a little recipe booklet that I picked up in Hawaii. It is a true Hawaiian dish, according to my husband. He has eaten it all his life.

You will need a cleaver or heavy knife to cut the chicken (bones and all) into small pieces.

Serves 6.

- 1 3-pound chicken
- 2 tablespoons vegetable oil
- 3 tablespoons soy sauce
- 1 tablespoon sugar
- 1 teaspoon salt
- 1/2 teaspoon pepper
- 2 cups water
- 1 small package dried mushrooms (about 6)
- 2 onions, sliced
- 1 12-ounce can sliced bamboo shoots
- 1 bunch green onions, cut 1 inch long
- Hot cooked rice

Cut chicken in small pieces (about 2 to 2½ inches). Saute in oil until browned. Add soy sauce and all seasonings. Add water and cover. Simmer ½ hour.

Meanwhile soak mushrooms in water 15 minutes, drain, remove tough stems and cut into strips and add to chicken, along with the two sliced onions.

Ten minutes before serving, add sliced bamboo shoots and green onions.

Serve over the hot cooked rice.

❦ CHICKEN POT ROAST ❦
Hawaiian

This recipe came from my sister-in-law who has lived in Hawaii all her life. Believe it or not, pineapple is not used in every Hawaiian recipe - in fact it is used no more often there than anywhere else.

Serves 4 to 6.

- 3 pounds chicken thighs
- 1/2 teaspoon salt
- 1/4 cup soy sauce
- 1 tablespoon salad oil
- 1 tablespoon grated fresh ginger
- 1 tablespoon sherry or dry vermouth
- 1 cup water
- 1 cup fresh sliced mushrooms
- 1 pound snow peas
- 2 green onions, cut into 1-inch lengths
- 1 tablespoon soy sauce
- 1 teaspoon Ac'cent
- 1 tablespoon cornstarch, mixed with 2 tablespoons water
- 1 teaspoon brown sugar

Rub chicken pieces with salt and the 1/4 cup soy sauce; let stand 15 minutes. Heat oil in skillet and brown chicken well on all sides. Combine ginger, sherry and water and pour over chicken; cover and simmer 30 minutes or until chicken is tender. Add mushrooms the last 5 minutes of cooking time Transfer chicken to serving dish and keep warm.

Leave mushrooms in skillet, add snow peas and green onions and remaining ingredients, cook until sauce thickens, stirring occasionally. Pour over chicken and serve.

🐦 PARMESAN CHICKEN BREAST 🐦

Serves 2.

- 1 whole chicken breast, boned and halved
- 1/2 cup plus 1 tablespoon freshly grated Parmesan cheese
- 1/2 cup all-purpose flour
- 3 tablespoons unsalted butter
- 1/4 cup dry vermouth
- 2 thin slices ham

Preheat oven to 375°F.

Rinse chicken breast halves and pat dry. Dredge the chicken breast in 1/2 cup of the Parmesan cheese, patting the cheese into the flesh then dredge them in the flour, shaking off excess.

In a non-stick skillet just large enough to hold the chicken without crowding, heat the butter until the foam begins to subside and in it saute the chicken over moderately high heat until golden on each side. Transfer the chicken to a baking dish, pour the vermouth over it and sprinkle the chicken with the remaining Parmesan cheese. Top with a slice of ham.

Bake the chicken, covered loosely, in a preheated oven for 15 minutes.

CHICKEN WITH SWISS CHEESE AND PROSCIUTTO

Makes 4 servings.

- 4 boneless chicken breast halves, skinned
- Garlic powder
- Salt and pepper
- 4 thin slices prosciutto (Italian cured ham)*
- 4 thin slices Swiss cheese
- 1 egg, beaten to blend
- 1 cup dry bread crumbs
- 3 tablespoons butter, melted

Preheat oven to 400°F.

Place chicken between two pieces of waxed paper and flatten to thickness of ¼ inch using meat mallet, rolling pin or skillet. Season both sides of chicken with garlic powder, salt and pepper.

Fold each prosciutto slice in half and roll tightly. Roll 1 cheese slice around each prosciutto piece. Place cheese roll on 1 long side of chicken breast. Roll up jelly-roll fashion, tucking in ends. Secure with toothpick. Repeat with remaining chicken and cheese rolls. Dip each breast into egg to coat. Dredge in bread crumbs. Place in baking dish. Drizzle butter over. Bake until cooked through, about 20 minutes. Serve immediately.

*Prosciutto can be found in the deli section of your grocery store. You can use regular sliced ham as a substitute if you like.

❦ CHICKEN PARMIGIANA ❦

Serve this to your new in-laws and impress them!!!! If you can cook something this good, they'll know their son or daughter is being well taken care of.

Serves 6.

- 3 whole chicken breasts, split, skinned and boned
- 2 eggs, lightly beaten
- 1 teaspoon salt
- 1/8 teaspoon pepper
- 3/4 cup fine dry bread crumbs
- 1/2 cup vegetable oil
- 2 8-ounce cans tomato sauce
- 1/4 teaspoon crumbled dried basil
- 1/8 teaspoon garlic powder
- 1 tablespoon butter
- 1/2 cup grated Parmesan cheese
- 8 ounces Mozzarella cheese, sliced and cut into triangles

Preheat oven to 350°F.

Place chicken breast on cutting board and pound lightly with meat tenderizer, heavy knife or cleaver until about 1/2 inch thick. Combine eggs, salt and pepper. Dip chicken into egg mixture, then crumbs. Heat oil until very hot in a large skillet. Quickly brown chicken on both sides. Remove to a shallow baking dish.

Pour off excess fat from skillet. Stir in tomato sauce, basil and garlic powder; bring to boiling; simmer for 10 minutes or until slightly thickened. Stir in the butter. Pour over chicken; sprinkle with Parmesan cheese; cover. Bake in preheated oven for 30 minutes. Uncover. Place mozzarella over chicken. Bake 10 minutes longer or until cheese melts.

PORTUGUESE CHICKEN

The Portuguese may not claim this dish but it is excellent.

Serves 3 to 4.

- 3 tablespoons butter or more
- 1 2-pound fryer, cut up
- 1 tablespoon chopped onion
- 1 tablespoon flour
- 1 clove garlic, minced
- 1/4 cup dry white wine or dry vermouth
- 1/2 cup chicken broth
- 1/2 cup canned tomatoes, drained and chopped
- Salt and pepper to taste
- 2 fresh tomatoes, peeled and chopped
- Chopped fresh parsley

In a large skillet heat the butter, add the chicken and brown on all sides. Remove chicken and keep hot. Add the onion to skillet and cook slowly, stirring constantly, three or four minutes. Add the flour and garlic and, stirring with a wire whisk, add the wine and broth and cook until the mixture is thickened and smooth. Add the canned tomatoes, salt and pepper.

Return the chicken to the skillet, cover and simmer until tender, about 30 minutes. Remove the chicken from the skillet to a warm serving platter and keep hot. Add the fresh tomatoes to the skillet and simmer 15 minutes. Pour the sauce over the chicken and garnish with chopped parsley.

We like this served with hot cooked rice.

❦ BAKED DRUMSTICKS ❦

This is one of my husband's favorites, but then he has many.

Serves 4.

- 1/3 cup Dijon mustard
- 2 garlic cloves, crushed through a press
- 1 tablespoon Worcestershire sauce
- 1 tablespoon vegetable oil
- 1 1/2 teaspoons Tabasco sauce
- 1 teaspoon paprika
- 8 chicken drumsticks, skin slashed at 1/2-inch intervals

In a small bowl, combine the mustard, garlic, Worcestershire sauce, oil, hot sauce and paprika; mix well.

Dip each drumstick in the sauce and arrange in a shallow glass dish. Pour any extra sauce over the chicken. Cover with plastic wrap and marinate in the refrigerator for at least 2 or up to 48 hours. Let the chicken return to room temperature before cooking.

Preheat oven to 375°F.

Bake the chicken uncovered for about 35 minutes or until the outside is browned and the juices run clear when the thickest part is pricked to the bone.

Preheat the broiler.

Broil the drumsticks 4 inches from the heat for about 2 minutes on each side to crisp the skin. Serve warm.

🌶 CHICKEN AND PASTA IN CREAM SAUCE 🌶

Paul Prudhomme puts out a group of seasonings called Cajun Magic. They are superb and I use them constantly. The next three recipes are from a small recipe booklet that Paul Prudhomme put out in conjunction with these spices. They are excellent and easy to prepare.

Serves 2.

- 1/3 pound uncooked dry spaghetti (thin)
- 6 tablespoons unsalted butter
- 1 tablespoon Paul Prudhomme's Cajun Magic Poultry Magic Seasoning Mix
- 1/2 pound, boneless, skinless chicken breast, diced
- 1/4 cup finely chopped green onions
- 2 cups heavy cream or half and half (I only use 1 cup - Sorry Paul!)

Cook spaghetti according to package directions just to al dente stage (tender, but not soft). Immediately drain and rinse with hot water to wash off starch, then with cold water to stop cooking process; drain again. To prevent pasta from sticking together, pour a very small amount of oil in palm of your hand and rub through pasta.

In large skillet, melt butter over medium heat. Add Poultry Magic Seasoning and chicken; saute about 1 minute, stirring occasionally. Add green onions and saute 1 to 2 minutes, continuing to stir. Gradually add cream, shaking pan in back-and-forth motion or stirring, until mixture boils. Reduce heat. Simmer until sauce thickens somewhat, continuing to shake pan, 2 to 3 minutes. Add cooked spaghetti; toss and stir until spaghetti is heated through, about 2 minutes. Serve immediately.

❦ CHICKEN DIANE ❦

Serves 2.

- 6 ounces uncooked dry pasta
- 3/4 cup (1 1/2 sticks) unsalted butter, divided
- 1 tablespoon plus 2 teaspoons Paul Prudhomme's Cajun Magic Poultry Magic Seasoning Mix
- 3/4 pound boneless, skinless chicken breast, cut into strips
- 3 cups sliced mushrooms (about 8 ounces)
- 1/4 cup minced green onion tops
- 3 tablespoons minced parsley
- 1 teaspoon minced garlic
- 1 cup chicken stock or water (I only use 1/2 cup)

Cook pasta according to package directions just to al dente stage (tender, but not soft). Immediately drain and rinse with hot water to wash off starch, then with cold water to stop cooking process; drain again. To prevent pasta from sticking together, pour a very small amount of oil in palm of your hand and rub through pasta.

Mash 4 tablespoons of the butter in medium bowl and combine with Poultry Magic Seasoning and chicken. Heat large skillet over heat until hot, about 4 minutes. Add chicken pieces and brown, about 2 minutes on first side and about 1 minute on the other. Add mushrooms and cook 2 minutes. Add green onions, parsley, garlic and stock. Cook 2 minutes more or until sauce is boiling rapidly. Add remaining butter (cut into pats) stirring and shaking pan to incorporate. Cook 3 minutes and add cooked pasta. Stir and shake pan to mix well. Serve immediately.

❦ BRONZED CHICKEN BREAST ❦

Serves 8.

> ¾ cup unsalted butter
> 8 boneless, skinless chicken breast halves, *well chilled*
> 1 tablespoon plus 2 teaspoons Paul Prudhomme's Cajun Magic Poultry Magic Seasoning Mix

Heat heavy griddle or large, heavy aluminum skillet to 350°F, about 7 minutes (½-inch flame) on gas stove, about 2 to 3 minutes over medium to medium-low heat on an electric stove. Or use an electric skillet. Heat 4 serving plates in 250°F oven.

Melt butter in a pie or cake pan. When griddle or skillet is heated, coat one chilled chicken breast half with warm melted butter. (DO NOT LAY IT DOWN ON SURFACE.) Sprinkle chicken breast evenly with about ½ teaspoon Poultry Magic Seasoning Mix; lay chicken on hot griddle or skillet surface. If you lay buttered and/or buttered and seasoned chicken down on plate or counter, butter - and seasonings as well - will adhere to plate or counter. Continue this procedure for remaining chicken. Set aside remaining melted butter.

Cook chicken until underside is bronzed in color, 4 to 5 minutes. Turn chicken and drizzle about ½ tablespoon melted butter down length of each breast. Cook until done, 4 to 5 minutes. Serve immediately on heated plates, allowing 1 breast half per person.

🦃 TURKEY MORNAY 🦃

This is a great way to use up leftover turkey.

Serves 4 to 6.

SAUCE:

- 4 tablespoons butter, divided
- 3 tablespoons flour
- 3/4 cup chicken broth
- 3/4 cup cream
- 2 egg yolks, slightly beaten
- 1/2 cup grated Gruyere cheese, plus some to sprinkle on top

Heat 3 tablespoons butter in top of double boiler over low heat and stir in flour until blended. Keep heating until mixture bubbles. Remove from heat and gradually stir in the chicken broth and cream. Return to heat and bring rapidly to boiling, stirring constantly; cook 1 to 2 minutes longer. Remove from heat and vigorously stir about 3 tablespoons sauce into egg yolks. Immediately return mixture to double boiler. Cook over simmering water 3 to 4 minutes. Cool slightly. Add cheese and the last tablespoon of butter at one time and blend until cheese melts.

Butter
Sliced English muffins
Leftover sliced turkey
Grated Gruyere cheese

Butter English muffins and toast in oven. Lay warmed turkey on muffins and pour generous amount of sauce overall; sprinkle more cheese over top and slip under broiler to brown just before serving.

❦ HOT 'N SAUCY TURKEY SANDWICHES ❦

Luncheon fare or "leftover" dinner.

Makes 4 generous servings.

- 3 tablespoons butter
- 3 tablespoons flour
- 1/2 teaspoon salt
- 1/2 teaspoon dry mustard
- 2 cups milk
- 1 cup shredded sharp Cheddar cheese
- 8 1/2-inch slices Italian bread, toasted
- 8 slices cooked white-meat turkey
- 1 10-ounce package frozen broccoli spears, cooked and drained
- 2 tablespoons crumbled blue cheese
- Paprika

In a medium saucepan melt butter; remove from heat; stir in flour, salt and mustard until smooth. Over medium heat gradually stir in milk. Cook, stirring, until slightly thickened. Stir in Cheddar cheese until melted and smooth; remove from heat.

In a large shallow broiler-proof dish, arrange toast in single layer; top with turkey and broccoli. Pour cheese sauce over all; sprinkle with blue cheese and paprika. Broil 3 inches from heat for 5 minutes or until sauce is lightly browned and bubbly. Serve immediately.

❦ SWISS TURKEY HAM BAKE ❦

This is an excellent way to use up leftover turkey and ham. It is elegant enough to serve to your fussiest guest.

Serves 6.

- 1/2 cup chopped onion
- 2 tablespoons butter
- 3 tablespoons flour
- 1/2 teaspoon salt
- 1/4 teaspoon black pepper
- 1 4-ounce can mushrooms, with juice
- 1 cup light cream
- 2 tablespoons dry sherry or dry vermouth
- 2 cups cooked turkey, cubed bite-size
- 1 cup cooked ham, cubed bite-size
- 1 5-ounce can sliced water chestnuts, drained
- 1/2 cup shredded Swiss cheese
- 1 1/2 cups soft bread crumbs
- 3 tablespoons melted butter

Preheat oven to 400°F.

Saute onions in butter. Blend in flour, salt and pepper. Add mushrooms, cream and sherry. Cook until slightly thickened. Add turkey, ham and chestnuts. Turn into a baking dish. Top with shredded Swiss cheese and bread crumbs that have been tossed in the melted butter. Bake for 20 minutes.

❧ HOT CHICKEN SUPREME ❧
Casserole

You can use turkey if you like. Another good way to use up the leftover Thanksgiving bird.

- 3 whole chicken breasts, cooked and diced
- 1½ cups chopped celery
- 1 cup shredded sharp Cheddar cheese
- 1 cup mayonnaise
- ¼ cup milk
- ¼ cup slivered almonds, toasted
- ¼ cup chopped pimento
- 2 tablespoons dry sherry or dry vermouth
- 2 teaspoons chopped onion
- ½ teaspoon poultry seasoning
- ½ teaspoon grated lemon rind
- 1 3-ounce can Chinese noodles

Preheat oven to 350°F.

Combine all ingredients except noodles; stir well. Spoon chicken mixture into a *greased* 1½-quart casserole and top with noodles. Bake for 30 minutes.

❦ NO PEEK CHICKEN ❦

The very name of this recipe tells you that it is no trouble at all to make.

Makes 4 to 6 servings.

- 1 6-ounce package Uncle Ben's long grain and wild rice mix
- 1 can cream of mushroom soup
- 1 can cream of celery soup
- 2 cups water
- 1/2 package onion soup mix (mix well before dividing)
- 6 pieces of chicken breasts or thighs

Preheat oven to 350°F.

Mix all ingredients, except chicken, in a large bowl. Put 2 cups of mixture in the bottom of a 12x9 baking dish. Add chicken pieces. Cover with the rest of the mixture. Cover tightly with foil. Bake for 2 hours.

NOTE: No salt is needed. The onion soup mix is salty enough.

🐓 BROILED CHICKEN 🐓

This is better still if cooked on outside charcoal or gas grill.

Serves 4 to 6.

- 3 to 3½ pound whole chicken, halved or quartered
- ¼ cup (½ stick) butter or margarine, softened or melted
- 1 large clove garlic, crushed
- 1 tablespoon finely chopped parsley
- Salt to taste

Clean and dry chicken. Combine butter, garlic and parsley. Place chicken on broiler rack. Salt chicken, then brush generously with the butter mixture. Broil about 3 inches from heat. Turn 3 to 4 times, brushing each time with butter mixture. Test for doneness by moving leg of chicken up and down. If it moves easily and the juices run clear when pricked with a fork, the chicken is done.

🐓 CHICKEN FRISCO 🐓

Serves 4.

- 1 4-ounce can mushrooms, drained
- 1 can mushroom soup
- 1 envelope spaghetti sauce mix
- 4 skinned chicken breast halves

Preheat oven to 350°F.

Mix the first three ingredients together. Place chicken breasts in a shallow pan. Pour sauce over chicken. Bake, uncovered, for 45 minutes.

❧ COUNTRY-STYLE CHICKEN KIEV ❧

This is a recipe from a butter advertisement. Don't overlook recipes in ads or on packages. If they were not good, the advertisers would not lend their names to them.

Serves 4.

- 2/3 cup unsalted butter
- 1/2 cup fine, dry bread crumbs
- 2 tablespoons grated Parmesan cheese
- 1 teaspoon each dried basil leaves and oregano
- 1/2 teaspoon garlic salt
- 1/4 teaspoon salt
- 2 whole chicken breasts, split
- 1/4 cup white wine or apple juice
- 1/4 cup chopped green onions
- 1/4 cup chopped fresh parsley

Preheat oven to 375°F.

Melt butter. Combine bread crumbs, Parmesan cheese, basil, oregano, garlic salt and salt. Dip chicken breast in melted butter, then coat with the crumb mixture; reserving the remaining butter. Place chicken, skin-side up, in an *ungreased*, 10-inch casserole dish. Bake for 50 minutes or until chicken is fork tender.

Meanwhile, add wine, green onion and parsley to reserved butter. When chicken is golden brown, pour butter mixture over chicken. Continue baking for 3 to 5 minutes or until sauce is heated through. Serve with sauce spooned over chicken.

🐓 CHICKEN BREAST - EDEN ISLE 🐓

A few years ago this recipe made the rounds under several different names and with slight variations in the ingredients. It really is a great dish, but some cooks find a good recipe and burn out on it by using it too often. I know I am guilty of this.

This recipe serves 12, so cut it down to meet your needs.

- 6 chicken breasts, boned and split
- Pepper
- 12 slices bacon
- 1 package of dried beef (not corned)
- 2 cans cream of chicken soup
- 1½ cups sour cream
- 3 ounces cream cheese, softened
- 6 to 8 cups hot cooked rice

Preheat oven to 325°F.

Pepper, but do not salt, chicken breasts. Wrap 1 slice of bacon around each breast. Place a layer of dried beef in the bottom of a baking dish. Arrange bacon-wrapped chicken breasts on the beef slices. Combine chicken soup, sour cream and cream cheese; pour over chicken. Cover the pan tightly with foil. Bake for 2 hours. When meat is tender, remove foil and let brown slightly. Serve on a bed of hot cooked rice.

❦ CHICKEN ELEGANT ❦

A favorite of my favorite son-in-law.

Serves 8.

- 4 whole boneless chicken breast, split
- 1/3 cup Dijon mustard
- 1 teaspoon dried dillweed or 1 tablespoon chopped fresh dill
- 1/4 pound Swiss cheese slices
- 2 frozen puff pastry sheets, thawed
- 1 egg
- 1 tablespoon cool water

Preheat oven to 375°F.

Between 2 sheets of waxed paper, pound chicken breast to 1/2-inch thickness. In small bowl, blend mustard and dill; spread on prepared chicken breast. Top each with cheese slices; roll up. Roll each pastry sheet to 12-inch square; cut each into 4 (6-inch) squares.

In small bowl, beat egg and water. Brush edges of each pastry square lightly with egg mixture. Place 1 chicken roll diagonally on each pastry square. Join 4 points of pastry over chicken; seal seams. Place on an *ungreased* baking sheet. Brush with remaining egg mixture. Bake for 30 minutes or until browned.

SEAFOOD

Most all seafood, especially shellfish, has become very expensive in the past few years. However, it is so good and so good for you that you should serve it often.

🌶 LOUISIANA STYLE BAKED SHRIMP 🌶

Served with a crusty Italian bread and a tossed salad, this makes a great meal!

Serves 2.

- ³/₄ pound shrimp, shelled and de-veined
- 3 tablespoons unsalted butter
- 1 teaspoon chili powder
- 1 teaspoon black pepper
- ¹/₈ teaspoon cayenne
- 1 teaspoon minced garlic
- 2 teaspoons Worcestershire sauce
- 2 tablespoons dry red wine

Preheat oven to 400°F.

Arrange the shrimp in a baking dish just large enough to hold them in one layer. In a small saucepan combine butter, chili powder, black pepper, cayenne, garlic, Worcestershire sauce, wine and salt and bring the mixture to a boil, pour it over the shrimp. Bake the shrimp in oven for 8 to 10 minutes or until they are just firm.

🦐 SHRIMP CASSEROLE 🦐

This is one of the best dishes I've ever found. Many years ago, a friend of mine used it as her recipe in the "Mrs. Georgia Pageant" (cooking was one of the categories). She came in second and I got the recipe from her.

This dish will not freeze, nor is it a very good leftover. The mayonnaise tends to turn back to its original oily state.

Serves 6.

- 2 pounds *cooked* shrimp, shelled and deveined
- 1 cup mayonnaise
- 1/4 cup finely chopped onions
- 1 1/2 cups finely chopped celery
- 1/2 teaspoon salt
- 1 tablespoon Worcestershire sauce
- 2 cups crushed potato chips
- Paprika

Preheat oven to 400°F.

Cut shrimp in half or thirds, making them bite-size. Mix shrimp well with mayonnaise, onions, celery, salt and Worcestershire sauce. Turn into a casserole dish and top with potato chips. Sprinkle with paprika. Bake for 20 to 25 minutes or until golden brown. The celery will still be crunchy.

You can cut the recipe in half if serving fewer people.

🦐 SHRIMP CREOLE 🦐

Serves 6 to 8.

- 3 pounds medium-sized shrimp
- 12 tomatoes, peeled and seeded or 4 cups canned tomatoes
- 1/2 cup vegetable oil
- 2 cups chopped onions
- 1 cup chopped green pepper
- 1 cup chopped celery
- 2 teaspoons minced garlic
- 1 cup water
- 2 bay leaves
- 1 tablespoon paprika
- 1/2 teaspoon cayenne pepper
- 1 teaspoon salt
- 2 tablespoons cornstarch, mixed with 1/4 cup cold water

Shell the shrimp and de-vein. Wash the shrimp and spread on paper towels to drain. Chop tomatoes and set aside.

In a heavy 4 to 5-quart dutch oven, heat the oil over moderate heat until a light haze forms above it. Add the onions, green peppers, celery and garlic and, stirring frequently, cook for about 5 minutes or until the vegetables are soft and translucent but not brown.

Stir in the tomatoes, water, bay leaves, paprika, cayenne and salt and bring to a boil. Reduce the heat to low, cover the dutch oven partially and, stirring occasionally, simmer the mixture for 20 to 25 minutes. Stir in the shrimp and continue to simmer, partially covered, for about 5 minutes longer or until the shrimp is pink and firm.

Stir in the cornstarch mixture. Stir over low heat for 2 to 3 minutes until sauce thickens slightly. Serve with hot cooked rice.

❦ VELVET SHRIMP ❦

Paul Prudhomme's Cajun Magic seasonings are outstanding and I use them often. This recipe is from a recipe booklet he published using these seasonings.

Serves 4.

- 3 tablespoons unsalted butter
- 1/2 cup finely chopped green onion tops
- 1 tablespoon plus 1 teaspoon Paul Prudhomme's Cajun Magic Seafood Magic Seasoning Mix
- 1/2 teaspoon minced garlic
- 1 pound medium to large shrimp, shelled and de-veined
- 2 cups heavy cream, divided (I use only 1 cup)
- 2 tablespoons seafood stock or water (you can use bottled clam juice)
- 1 cup shredded Muenster cheese (4 ounces)
- Hot cooked pasta or rice

Melt butter in 10-inch skillet over high heat. When it comes to a hard sizzle, stir in green onions and 1 tablespoon of the Seafood Magic Seasoning. Cook about 1 1/2 minutes then add garlic and shrimp. Cook about 2 minutes, stirring, then add 1 cup of the cream and the remaining Seafood Magic Seasoning. Stir and scrape any browned bits off sides and bottom of skillet. Cook about 1 minute and stir in remaining cream. Cook 1 minute or just until shrimp are plump and pink; remove with slotted spoon. Set aside. Still over high heat, whisk cream mixture often as it comes to a boil, then whisk constantly. Cook, whisking, 2 or 3 minutes, then add stock and cheese. Cook 1 minute more or until cheese has melted. Return shrimp to skillet. Stir to coat shrimp with sauce. Serve over pasta or rice.

🦌 SHRIMP EGG FOO YONG 🦌

As you can see, there are several Chinese and other Oriental recipes in this collection. Why not make several of them and have a real ethnic dinner?

SAUCE:

- 4 teaspoons soy sauce
- 2 teaspoons cornstarch
- 2 teaspoons sugar
- 2 teaspoons vinegar
- 1½ teaspoons salt
- 1 cup cold water

EGG FOO YONG:

- 1½ cups fresh bean sprouts
- ⅔ cup thinly sliced onions
- 1 cup drained, cooked shrimp, coarsely cut up
- 6 eggs
- 2 tablespoons bacon fat or salad oil

About 50 minutes before serving, make sauce. In saucepan, combine soy sauce, cornstarch, sugar, vinegar and salt. Stir in water and cook over low heat until thickened. Set aside.

Combine bean sprouts with onions and shrimp. Then, with fork, beat eggs. Add bean sprout mixture to eggs. In hot skillet, heat oil and fry, as a pancake, about ½ cup mixture at a time, turning once. Fold pancake over; keep hot until all mixture is cooked. Arrange on hot platter. Cover with heated sauce.

🦐 PINEAPPLE SHRIMP 🦐

This recipe came from a little cookbook I picked up in Hawaii. It brings rave notices when I serve it to guests.

Serves 4.

SAUCE:

- 1 cup sugar
- 2 cups canned pineapple chunks
- 1 cup tomato paste
- 2 teaspoons salt
- 2 cups pineapple juice
- 1 cup vinegar
- 2 cups water
- 1 green pepper, cut into large chunks
- 1 small onion, cut into large chunks

Combine the sauce ingredients in a saucepan; bring to a boil and remove from heat.

SHRIMP:

- 1 cup flour
- 1/2 teaspoon sugar
- 1/2 teaspoon salt
- 1 egg
- 1 cup ice water
- 1 pound fresh shrimp
- 2 cups oil for frying

In a bowl, mix flour, sugar, salt, egg and ice water to make a smooth batter.

Peel shrimp, leaving last section and tail intact. Slit lengthwise and remove vein. Dry shrimp thoroughly.

Dip in batter and deep-fry in hot oil for 2 to 3 minutes. Drain on paper towels.

Thicken sauce with 2 tablespoons cornstarch mixed with ½ cup water. Bring to a boil. Remove from heat and pour over shrimp. Serve with hot cooked rice.

🦐 TEMPURA SHRIMP 🦐

The batter for this is good as a batter for fried zucchini, eggplant or any food you batter and fry. If you use it on chicken, the pieces should be small - like chicken breast cut into cubes.

Prepare batter just before using. Makes about 1¼ cups.

- 1 cup cake flour
- 2 tablespoons cornstarch
- 2 teaspoons baking powder
- ½ teaspoon salt
- 2 egg whites
- ¾ cup ice water
- Shrimp

Combine cake flour, cornstarch, baking powder and salt. Add egg whites and water and blend, mixing just until flour is incorporated. (Batter should be the consistency of whipping cream; if too thick, add more ice water. Batter may have small lumps.) Transfer to a small bowl; set inside larger bowl filled with ice. Use immediately.

If you have a food processor, put cake flour, cornstarch, baking powder and salt in work bowl and mix 2 seconds. Add egg whites and water and blend using 4 or 5 on/off turns, mixing just until flour is incorporated.

Dip cleaned, shelled shrimp into batter; let excess drip off. Fry in very hot oil for 2 to 3 minutes. Drain on paper towels.

❦ SUPERB SEAFOOD CASSEROLE ❦

As I try new recipes they are given one of three ratings - very good, excellent or superb - all others are trashed. This rates superb.

Makes 6 servings.

- 3/4 pound cleaned shrimp
- 3/4 pound bay scallops
- 4 tablespoons melted butter
- 1/4 cup all-purpose flour
- 1 teaspoon salt
- Dash of black pepper
- 1 1/2 cups milk
- 2 tablespoons dry sherry
- 1/2 pound crabmeat (use fresh, frozen or canned)
- 1 1/2 cups soft bread crumbs
- 1/4 cup shredded Cheddar cheese
- 2 tablespoons melted butter
- Paprika

Preheat oven to 350°F.

Cut large shrimp in half. Saute shrimp and scallops in 4 tablespoons butter in a large saucepan over medium heat for 4 to 6 minutes or until opaque. Remove shrimp and scallops from pan, reserving butter in pan. Stir flour, salt and pepper into reserved butter and blend well. Add milk gradually and cook over low heat, stirring constantly, until thickened. Stir in sherry. Fold in crabmeat, shrimp and scallops.

Spoon into 6 individual baking shells or ramekins (individual casserole dishes). You can use one eight-cup casserole instead of individual dishes.

Combine bread crumbs, cheese and 2 tablespoons melted butter; sprinkle over seafood mixture. Bake for 10 to 15 minutes or until heated thoroughly. Sprinkle with paprika.

❦ BROOK TROUT STUFFED WITH CRABMEAT ❦

Superb! This is quite an expensive dish, but, boy, will it impress the boss! It takes a little time, but is not difficult to make.

Serves 6, allowing one fish per person.

- 6 brook trout, about 8 ounces each
- 1 stick butter (¼ pound), divided
- ¼ cup finely chopped shallots
- 6 tablespoons dry white wine
- ½ cup finely chopped mushrooms
- 1½ cups cooked crabmeat
- 3 tablespoons flour
- 6 tablespoons clam juice
- 6 tablespoons heavy cream
- 3 egg yolks
- 1 tablespoon finely chopped parsley
- ¼ teaspoon salt
- ⅛ teaspoon white pepper
- Olive oil

Preheat oven to 325°F.

TO MAKE STUFFING: Melt ½ stick butter in a 10-inch skillet, over low heat. Add shallots; cook until tender. Add wine and mushrooms; cook until liquid evaporates. Stir in crabmeat and set skillet aside.

In a 1-quart saucepan, melt remaining butter over low heat. Stir in flour and blend well with a wire whisk. Cook 1 minute. Add clam juice and cream; stirring constantly, cooking until mixture thickens and comes to a boil. Beat egg yolks in small bowl. Beat into the egg yolks a little of the hot clam sauce mixture. Slowly add yolk mixture to saucepan, beating constantly. Cook, stirring constantly, until mixture thickens slightly; do not allow to boil. Add parsley, salt and pepper. Blend sauce into crabmeat mixture and keep warm in a double boiler over barely simmering water.

Combine 4 tablespoons flour, $1/2$ teaspoon salt and $1/4$ teaspoon white pepper on a plate. Roll fish in flour mixture to coat well. Heat olive oil $1/2$-inch deep in a heavy skillet until a light haze forms. Saute trout, two at a time, until golden brown, about 2 to 3 minutes on each side. Divide stuffing and stuff each fish.

Put fish in shallow baking dish. Cover with foil and bake for about 20 minutes. Drizzle with hot, melted butter.

🦐 FLOUNDER WITH SHRIMP SAUCE 🦐

Serves 2.

- 4 tablespoons butter, divided
- 2 teaspoons all-purpose flour
- 1/2 cup milk
- 3 tablespoons dry sherry
- Salt and freshly ground pepper
- 1 small can shrimp, drained
- 4 large mushrooms, sliced
- 1 green onion, diced
- 2 tablespoons finely chopped parsley
- Pinch of dried dillweed
- Pinch of paprika
- Pinch of dried rosemary, crumbled
- 2 teaspoons butter
- Juice of 1/2 lemon
- 2 flounder fillets (about 3/4 pounds)

Melt 2 tablespoons butter in heavy small saucepan over low heat. Stir in flour and cook 3 minutes. Add milk and sherry. Increase heat to medium high and continue cooking, stirring constantly, until sauce boils and is moderately thick. Season with salt and freshly ground pepper. Set aside and keep warm.

Melt 2 tablespoons butter in heavy large skillet over medium-high heat. Add mushrooms, green onions, parsley, dillweed, paprika, rosemary, salt and pepper and saute until onions are soft. Add drained shrimp. Remove shrimp mixture from skillet.

Melt remaining 2 teaspoons butter in same skillet over medium heat. Stir in lemon juice. Add flounder and cook until fish turns opaque, about 1 to 2 minutes per side. Season with salt and pepper. Arrange fillets on heated platter. Spoon half of shrimp mixture over fillets. Whisk fish cooking liquid into white sauce and pour over fish. Spoon remaining shrimp over top. We like this served with rice pilaf.

❦ BROILED MONKFISH ❦

This fish is so ugly in appearance in the fish market that it was overlooked for years. When the price of fish went sky-high, someone took a chance on monkfish, because it was cheap and discovered it to be delicious. In fact, it has been called the poor man's lobster. I would not go quite that far, but it is good.

Preheat oven to 400°F.

Fillet fish not more than ¾-inch thick. Then paint it with a mixture of pureed garlic, salt, lemon juice, oil, thyme, rosemary and oregano (or any herb mixture). Let it marinade for an hour or more before cooking.

Broil close to heating element for 5 minutes or so, then bake for another 10 minutes, basting with white wine or dry vermouth.

GRILLED SALMON WITH MUSTARD DILL SAUCE

Serves 4.

    1½ pounds salmon fillets
        Paul Prudhomme's Cajun Seafood Magic Seasoning

Mustard Dill Sauce (makes 2½ cups):

    ½ cup sugar
    1 cup fresh dill or ¼ cup dried dillweed
    1 cup Dijon mustard
    ⅓ cup wine vinegar
    ½ cup mayonnaise
    2 tablespoons vegetable oil

Combine all sauce ingredients in a blender or processor. Blend until mixture is smooth. Set aside.

Sprinkle fillets very generously with the seafood seasoning. Let stand about 15 minutes.

Heat outdoor grill (charcoal, gas or electric). Cook fillets until fish flakes easily. Serve with the sauce.

❦ BAKED OYSTERS WITH BREAD CRUMBS AND GARLIC ❦

This recipe came from an Italian cookbook, so I assume it is Italian.

Serves 4 to 6.

- 2 tablespoons butter
- 1 cup fresh bread crumbs
- 1 teaspoon finely chopped garlic
- 2 tablespoons chopped parsley
- 2 dozen oysters, shucked*
- 3 tablespoons grated Parmesan cheese
- 2 tablespoons butter, cut into tiny pieces

Preheat oven to 450°F.

Butter an 8x10 or 8x12-inch baking dish.

In a heavy 8-inch skillet, melt 2 tablespoons butter. Add the fresh bread crumbs and the garlic and toss them in the butter until they are crisp and golden. Stir in the parsley. Spread about ⅔ cup of the bread crumb mixture in the bottom of the buttered baking dish and arrange oysters over it in one layer. Mix the rest of the bread crumb mixture with the grated cheese and spread the combination on the oysters. Dot with bits of butter.

Bake the oysters for 12 to 15 minutes until golden.

*You can buy fresh oysters already shucked at the fish market.

❦ CRAB-FILLED JUMBO MUSHROOMS ❦

This is a main dish version of the traditional appetizer of stuffed mushrooms. It sometimes takes some searching to find jumbo mushrooms. You can use fresh, frozen or canned crabmeat. If frozen, thaw and drain. If canned, drain.

Serves 4.

- 1 6-ounce package Uncle Ben's long grain and wild rice mix
- 8 large jumbo mushrooms (1 pound)
- 4 tablespoons butter or margarine, divided
- 2 green onions, minced (about 1/4 cup)
- 1 tablespoon all-purpose flour
- 1/8 teaspoon pepper
- 3/4 cup milk
- 2 cups white bread cubes (4 slices)
- 1 tablespoon dry sherry or dry vermouth
- 6 ounces Alaska King or Snow crab
- 1/2 cup shredded Cheddar cheese
- 4 ounces Mozzarella cheese, cut into 8 slices
- 1 tablespoon minced parsley

Preheat oven to 425°F.

Prepare rice as label directs; keep warm.

Remove stems from mushrooms. Set mushroom caps aside. Dice and reserve stems.

In a 12-inch skillet, over medium heat, melt 2 tablespoons butter; add mushroom caps and cook 5 minutes, turning caps once. With slotted spoon, remove caps to an 8x8-inch baking dish or pan.

In same skillet over medium heat, melt 2 more tablespoons butter; add green onions and reserved mushroom stems and cook until tender, stirring occasionally. Stir in flour and pepper until blended.

Gradually stir in milk and cook, stirring constantly, until mixture is slightly thickened and smooth. Stir in bread cubes, sherry, crabmeat and Cheddar cheese. Remove from heat.

Spoon some crabmeat filling into each mushroom cap, shaping into a high mound. Bake 10 minutes or until hot. Top each mushroom with a slice of Mozzarella cheese and bake about 3 minutes longer or until cheese is melted.

TO SERVE: Spoon rice mixture onto warm platter. Arrange mushrooms on rice; sprinkle mushrooms with parsley.

🦀 CHESAPEAKE CRAB CAKES 🦀

Crabmeat is so expensive now. I found I could use canned lump crabmeat and get excellent results. The original recipe called for 1 pound of fresh cooked crab, but I use 12 ounces of the canned.

Serves 6.

- 1 cup fresh bread crumbs
- 1/2 cup mayonnaise
- 1/4 cup minced fresh parsley
- 1 large egg, lightly beaten
- 2 teaspoons Worcestershire sauce
- 1 teaspoon Old Bay seafood seasoning
- 1/4 teaspoon each cayenne and dry mustard
- Salt and pepper to taste
- 2 6-ounce cans lump crabmeat
- Fresh bread crumbs for dusting crab cakes
- 3 tablespoons vegetable oil

In a large bowl combine 1 cup bread crumbs, mayonnaise, parsley, egg, Worcestershire, Old Bay seasoning, cayenne, dry mustard and salt and pepper. Fold in the crabmeat gently; form the mixture into 6 balls and flatten the balls into 3-inch cakes. Dust the cakes with bread crumbs and chill them on a plate, covered loosely, for 1 hour.

In a large skillet heat oil over moderately high heat until it is hot. Saute the cakes in batches, adding more oil if necessary, for 2 to 3 minutes on each side or until they are golden brown, transferring them with a slotted spatula as they are cooked to heated platter. Serve the crab cakes with lemon wedges.

❦ POOR MAN'S CRAB CASSEROLE ❦

Serves 4.

    1 1-pound package frozen cod fillets (not breaded), thawed and drained

CRAB MIXTURE:

- 2/3 cup unsalted butter, melted
- 2 tablespoons chopped, fresh parsley
- 1 cup crushed herb-seasoned stuffing mix
- 6 ounces crabmeat (if frozen or canned, drain well)
- 1 egg
- 1/4 teaspoon salt
- 2 tablespoons lemon juice
- 1/4 teaspoon Tabasco hot sauce
- 1 4-ounce can mushroom stems and pieces, drained

TOPPING:

- 1/2 cup crushed herb-seasoned stuffing mix
- 2 tablespoons unsalted butter, melted

Preheat oven to 350°F.

In an *ungreased* 8-inch square baking dish, place cod fillets. In 1½-quart bowl, mix together all crab mixture ingredients. Sprinkle crab mixture over cod fillets. In same bowl combine topping ingredients. Sprinkle over crab mixture. Bake for 30 to 35 minutes or until heated through and fish fillets flake easily.

FISH AND CHIP BAKE

An inexpensive casserole dish. If you like fish, you'll love this - even if you don't like spinach.

Serves 4.

- 4 servings instant mashed potatoes
- 1 10-ounce package frozen, chopped spinach, thawed and drained
- 1/2 cup sour cream
- Dash of pepper
- 1 16-ounce package frozen perch fillets, thawed
- 1/4 cup milk
- 1/2 cup herb-seasoned stuffing mix, crushed
- 2 tablespoons butter, melted
- Lemon slices for garnish

Preheat oven to 350°F.

Prepare potatoes according to package directions, except reduce water by 1/4 cup. Stir in drained spinach, sour cream and pepper. Turn into a 10x6x2-inch baking dish.

Skin fish fillets, if necessary. Dip one side of each fillet in milk, then in crushed stuffing mix. Fold fillets in half, coating side out. Place atop the potato mixture; drizzle with the melted butter.

Bake, uncovered, until fish flakes easily, about 30 minutes. Garnish with lemon slices.

❦ FILLETS OF SOLE IN CREOLE SAUCE ❦

Serves 4.

- 1 medium onion, chopped
- 1/2 cup celery, chopped
- 1 tablespoon butter
- 1 8-ounce can tomato sauce
- 1/2 teaspoon salt
- 1/2 teaspoon curry powder
- 1/8 teaspoon pepper
- 1 cup chopped green pepper
- 2 1-pound packages frozen fillets of sole

Partially thaw fish.

Saute onion and celery in butter until soft in a large skillet; stir in tomato sauce, salt, curry powder, pepper and green pepper. Cut each fish in thirds; place in single layer in sauce; cover. Bring to boiling, then simmer 15 minutes or until fish flakes easily. Serve with hot cooked rice.

SALMON FRITTERS

Makes about 24 patties.

- 1 16-ounce can salmon, drained and flaked
- 1 cup Bisquick baking mix
- 1 egg
- 1/2 teaspoon salt
- 1 tablespoon lemon juice
- 2 tablespoons sliced green onions (with tops)
- 2 tablespoons finely chopped green pepper
- 1 teaspoon dried dillweed
- Oil for frying

In deep fat fryer or kettle, heat 3 to 4 inches fat or oil to 365°F (hot).

Mix all ingredients; drop by rounded tablespoonfuls, a few at a time, into hot fat. Fry, turning once, until golden brown, about 2 minutes. Drain on paper toweling.

❧ TUNA BUNSTEADS ❧

These can be made ahead, wrapped individually in foil and frozen. To serve, thaw and bake.

Serves 8.

- 3 hard boiled eggs, chopped
- 1/2 small onion, chopped
- 1 6 1/2-ounce can tuna
- 1 cup chopped Velveeta cheese
- 1/4 cup chopped sweet pickles
- 1/4 cup chopped olives
- 1/4 cup chopped green peppers
- 1/2 to 3/4 cup mayonnaise
- 8 hamburger buns

Mix above ingredients, except buns, with mayonnaise. Spoon onto hamburger buns. Place buns in oven and cover with foil. Bake for 25 minutes.

SIDE DISHES

Vegetables, Potatoes, Rice and Such

Since you will probably serve a salad and a bread with most entrees, I decided that "Side Dishes" was the appropriate name for this section.

🌱 STEAMED VEGETABLES 🌱

An excellent way to cook a lot of vegetables such as green beans, carrots, peas, celery, zucchini, broccoli and cauliflower, is by simply steaming them and sprinkling with chicken bouillon granules. The granules are salty so you will not need any further seasoning. You can cook these vegetables alone or in any combination you like.

🌱 BAKED VIDALIA ONIONS 🌱

Vidalia onions are only available a few weeks out of the year. Grab them while you can and enjoy!

Serves 4.

- 4 Vidalia onions
- 1/2 stick (1/4 cup) unsalted butter
- 1/4 cup freshly grated Parmesan cheese
- Salt and pepper

Preheat oven to 400°F.

Peel onions and cut a 1/2-inch deep cone out of the top of each onion. Arrange the onions cut side up in a buttered baking pan just large enough to hold them in one layer. Put 1 tablespoon butter in the cavity of each onion and sprinkle the onions with the Parmesan cheese and salt and pepper. Add to the pan 1/4 inch water and bake the onions, covered with foil, for 55 minutes or until they are tender. Transfer the onions to a serving dish. Put the cooking liquid into a small saucepan and reduce over high heat to about 1/4 cup and spoon it over the onions.

❦ CARAWAY CABBAGE ❦

A very good side dish!

Serves 8.

>   2 tablespoons unsalted butter
>   1 pound cabbage quartered, cored and cut crosswise into ¼-inch strips
>   1 tablespoon caraway seeds
>   1 tablespoon distilled white vinegar
>   Salt

In a heavy skillet or kettle heat the butter over moderately high heat until the foam subsides. In it saute the cabbage, sprinkled with the caraway seeds and salt to taste. Toss it, for 1 to 2 minutes or until it is coated well with the butter. Cook the cabbage, covered, over moderate heat for 2 to 3 minutes or until just wilted. Transfer the cabbage to a heated serving dish. Sprinkle with the vinegar and toss again to mix.

CHEESY BROCCOLI CASSEROLE

Make this dish with asparagus when it's in season.

Serves 4 to 6.

- 1 1/2 pounds fresh broccoli
- 2 slightly beaten eggs
- 3/4 cup cottage cheese
- 1/2 cup shredded Cheddar cheese
- 2 tablespoons finely chopped onion
- 1 teaspoon Worcestershire sauce
- 1/2 teaspoon salt
- 1/8 teaspoon pepper
- 1/4 cup fine dry bread crumbs
- 1 tablespoon melted butter

Preheat oven to 350°F.

Wash and trim broccoli; cut stalks into spears. Cook broccoli, covered in a small amount of boiling water, about 10 minutes or until crisp-tender; drain. Meanwhile, in bowl combine eggs, cheeses, onion, Worcestershire sauce, salt and pepper. Arrange broccoli spears in a shallow 1 1/2-quart baking dish; spoon cheese mixture atop. Stir together bread crumbs and melted butter; sprinkle over cheese mixture. Bake, uncovered, for 15 to 20 minutes or until heated through and egg mixture is set. Serve immediately.

BROCCOLI MARINADE

Marvelous for buffets!

Makes 4 to 6 servings.

- 2 cups broccoli flowerets
- 1/2 cup vegetable oil
- 1/4 cup vinegar
- 1 teaspoon salt
- 1/4 teaspoon pepper
- 1 cup coarsely chopped red onion
- 1 cucumber, peeled, seeded and coarsely chopped
- 1 tomato, seeded and coarsely chopped
- 1 cup shredded Cheddar cheese

Blanch broccoli flowerets by dropping into boiling water for 2 minutes. Drain well. In small bowl, combine oil, vinegar, salt and pepper. Combine broccoli with onion, cucumber, tomato and cheese; toss in dressing to mix well. Marinate 2 to 3 hours in refrigerator, stirring occasionally.

❦ GLAZED CARROTS ❦

These are not only delicious, but they add color to the plate.

Serves 4 to 6.

- 10 to 12 carrots, peeled and cut into 2-inch pieces
- 1½ cups beef broth
- 4 tablespoons butter
- 2 tablespoons sugar
- ½ teaspoon salt
- Black pepper
- 2 tablespoons finely chopped parsley

In a heavy 8 to 10-inch skillet, bring the carrots, beef broth, butter, sugar, salt and a few grindings of black pepper to a boil over moderate heat. Then cover and simmer over low heat, shaking occasionally to roll the carrots about in the liquid. Check to see that the liquid is not cooking away too fast; if it is, add more broth. In 20 to 30 minutes the carrots should be tender and the braising liquid should be a brown, syrupy glaze. If the stock has not reduced enough, remove the carrots to a plate and boil the liquid down over high heat. Before serving, roll the carrots in liquid and transfer to serving dish. Garnish with parsley.

SWEET AND SOUR BEETS

These are basically the same as Harvard Beets.

Serves 2.

- 2 tablespoons sugar
- 1 teaspoon cornstarch
- 2 tablespoons water
- 2 tablespoons vinegar
- 1 tablespoon vegetable oil
- 1 16-ounce can sliced beets, drained
- 1/8 teaspoon salt
- Dash of pepper

Combine sugar and cornstarch in a saucepan; stir well. Gradually add water, stirring until smooth. Stir in vinegar and oil; cook over medium heat, stirring constantly until thickened. Add beets, salt and pepper; cook over medium heat 10 minutes or until thoroughly heated.

❧ RATATIOULE ❧
Vegetable Stew with Eggplant

Serves 8 to 10.

- 1 medium onion, sliced into thin wedges
- 2 cloves garlic, minced
- 1/4 cup olive oil
- 1 16-ounce can tomatoes, cut up
- 1 1/2 teaspoons dried thyme, crushed
- 1 teaspoon salt
- 1/4 teaspoon pepper
- 1 bay leaf
- 2 medium unpeeled eggplants
- 2 medium zucchini, cut into strips
- 1 green pepper, seeded and cut into strips

In a Dutch oven, cook onion and garlic in oil until tender. Add *undrained* tomatoes, thyme, salt, pepper and bay leaf. Cover; simmer 10 minutes. Discard bay leaf. Remove and set aside 2 cups of the sauce mixture. Slice eggplant in half lengthwise, then crosswise into 1/2-inch slices. Arrange half of eggplant, zucchini and pepper over sauce in pan. Sprinkle with salt and pepper. Cover with 1 cup reserved sauce. Arrange remaining vegetables atop; sprinkle with more salt and pepper. Pour over remaining sauce. Cover; simmer 20 minutes. Uncover and simmer 15 minutes longer. Serve hot or cold.

❧ FRIED EGGPLANT ❧

Serves 4.

- 1 large eggplant, peeled and cut into thin strips about ⅛-inch thick
- 2 tablespoons kosher salt
- 1 tablespoon lemon juice
- 2 quarts water
- 1 cup evaporated milk
- 1 cup self-rising flour (or as much as needed)
- Hot oil for deep frying

Combine salt, lemon juice and water. Soak eggplant in this overnight. Remove eggplant from marinade, rinse and dip in evaporated milk and lightly coat with flour. Deep fry pieces until golden brown.

❦ SAUTEED ZUCCHINI WITH CARROTS ❦

Good vegetable recipes are scarce. This is a very good one.

Serves 4.

- 5 or 6 carrots, peeled and sliced thin
- 2 tablespoons butter or margarine
- 1/4 cup thinly sliced small, white onions
- 2 small zucchini (about 3/4 pound), trimmed and sliced thin
- 1/2 teaspoon salt
- 1/4 teaspoon pepper
- 3 tablespoons fresh chopped or 1 tablespoon dried basil

In medium saucepan over medium heat, cook carrots in butter, stirring occasionally, 4 minutes. Add onions; cook and stir 1 minute. Add zucchini; cook, stirring and shaking pan, 1 minute. Add salt and pepper. Cover and cook 4 minutes or until vegetables are crisp-tender. Sprinkle with basil.

ZUCCHINI PARMESAN

Makes 8 servings.

- 2½ pounds zucchini, thinly sliced
- ⅔ cup chopped onion
- 1 cup sliced fresh mushrooms
- 3 tablespoons vegetable oil
- 2 6-ounce cans tomato paste
- ½ teaspoon garlic salt
- 1 teaspoon salt
- ⅛ teaspoon pepper
- ⅔ cup grated Parmesan cheese, divided

Preheat oven to 350°F.

Saute zucchini, onion and mushrooms in hot oil for 5 to 6 minutes, stirring occasionally. Remove from heat; stir in tomato paste, garlic salt, salt, pepper and ⅓ cup Parmesan cheese. Spoon into a 2-quart casserole dish; sprinkle with remaining cheese. Cover and bake for 30 minutes or until bubbly.

❦ SAUTEED SHREDDED ZUCCHINI ❦

This is a great vegetable dish and very quick and easy to do.

Serves 4 to 6.

- 4 medium zucchini, trimmed but not peeled
- 1 teaspoon salt
- 1 tablespoon unsalted butter
- 1 tablespoon olive oil
- 1 tablespoon chopped green onions with tops

Shred zucchini in food processor fitted with shredding disc, or grate by hand. Transfer zucchini to colander; sprinkle with salt, toss and allow to drain 25 minutes.

Heat butter and oil in 10-inch skillet over medium heat. When foam subsides, add green onions and saute until tender, about 2 minutes.

Press zucchini firmly with back of spoon to extract as much liquid as possible. Toss with butter mixture in skillet. Saute until zucchini is crisp-tender, about 3 minutes.

❧ ZUCCHINI STICKS ❧

Makes an excellent appetizer as well as a side dish.

Serves 4 to 6.

- 4 eggs
- 1/4 cup whipping cream
- 1/2 teaspoon freshly ground pepper
- 1/4 teaspoon salt
- 3 to 4 medium zucchini, quartered and cut into 2-inch lengths
- 3/4 cup seasoned bread crumbs (Progresso is good)
- Oil for deep frying

Mix eggs, cream, pepper and salt in blender (or beat together by hand). Transfer to bowl. Heat oil to 350°F (hot). Dip zucchini into egg mixture, then coat with bread crumbs. Add to oil in batches and fry until browned and crisp, about 3 to 4 minutes. Drain on paper towels. Serve hot.

❦ FRENCH-FRIED MUSHROOMS ❦

Can be served as an appetizer as well as a vegetable dish.

Serves 4.

- 1 egg
- 1/2 cup milk
- 1/3 cup all-purpose flour
- 1/2 teaspoon salt
- 20 medium-sized mushrooms
- 1 cup cornflakes, crushed
- Vegetable oil for frying
- Seasoned salt

Combine egg and milk, beating well. Stir together flour and salt. Dredge mushrooms in flour mixture then dip in egg mixture; roll in cornflake crumbs. Deep fry in hot oil (375°) until golden brown.

Drain on paper towels and sprinkle with seasoned salt. Serve immediately.

❦ GOLDEN PAN-FRIED MUSHROOMS ❦

Serves 4.

- 1 pound small mushrooms
- 1 egg, beaten
- 1/2 cup dry bread crumbs
- 1 medium onion, chopped
- 1/3 cup butter or margarine

Dip mushrooms into egg then coat with bread crumbs.

Cook mushrooms and onions in butter in 12-inch skillet, turning occasionally, until mushrooms are tender and golden, 7 to 8 minutes.

GREEN BEAN BAKE

Serves 6.

- 1½ pounds fresh green beans, trimmed or two 10-ounce packages frozen whole green beans
- 1 clove garlic, sliced
- ¼ teaspoon seasoned pepper*
- 8 ounces sour cream
- 2 tablespoons butter
- 1 cup soft bread crumbs

Preheat oven to 350°F.

Cook the beans with the garlic until tender or, if frozen, cook according to label directions; drain. Place in a 4-cup baking dish. Stir the seasoned pepper into sour cream and spoon over beans. Melt butter in small saucepan; add bread crumbs and toss to coat well. Sprinkle over sour cream.

Bake for 20 minutes or until crumbs are golden.

*This can be found in the spice section of your grocery store.

❦ STIR-FRIED SNOW PEAS ❦

If you are serving an Oriental dinner, be sure to include these.

Serves 4.

- 6 dried Chinese mushrooms*
- 1 pound fresh snow peas
- 2 tablespoons cooking oil
- 1/2 cup canned sliced bamboo shoots, drained
- 1 1/2 teaspoons salt
- 1/2 teaspoon sugar

In a small bowl, cover mushrooms with 1/2 cup warm water and let them soak for 30 minutes. Remove them with a slotted spoon. (Reserve the liquid.) Cut away and discard the tough stems. Cut each cap in quarters. Strain the reserved liquid and reserve 2 tablespoons of it.

Clean and string the snow peas.

Have the above ingredients and the oil, bamboo shoots, salt and sugar within easy reach.

Heat wok or heavy skillet over high heat. Pour in oil, swirl about in pan and heat for 30 seconds. Immediately drop in the mushrooms and bamboo shoots and stir-fry for 2 minutes. Add the snow peas, salt and sugar and the reserved liquid from the mushrooms. Cook, stirring constantly, for about 2 minutes or until liquid evaporates. Serve hot.

*Available in most supermarkets or at an Oriental store.

🦃 SUPERB VEGETABLE CASSEROLE 🦃

Delicious! But I would save this for a special occasion. No need to put this much effort into a Monday night dinner.

Serves 6 to 8.

- 2 cups small carrot sticks
- 2 cups small zucchini sticks
- 1/2 cup boiling water
- 1/2 teaspoon salt
- 1/2 cup butter, divided
- 2 tablespoons flour
- 1 1/2 cups half and half cream
- 2 crumbled chicken bouillon cubes
- 1/2 teaspoon prepared mustard
- 1/2 teaspoon dill weed, divided
- 1/16 teaspoon nutmeg (or a couple dashes)
- 1/16 teaspoon pepper (or a couple dashes)
- 1 6-ounce can tiny onions, drained
- 2 1/4 cup soft bread crumbs
- 3/4 cup grated Cheddar cheese
- 2/3 cup coarsely chopped walnuts

Preheat oven to 375°F.

Combine carrots, zucchini, water and salt; bring to a boil. Cover and cook 10 minutes. Drain well and set aside.

Melt 2 tablespoons butter and stir in flour. Gradually add half and half, bouillon, mustard and 1/4 teaspoon dill, nutmeg and pepper. Cook and stir until boiling.

Add carrots, zucchini and onions. Turn into shallow 7-cup baking dish.

Melt remaining butter and toss with crumbs, cheese, walnuts and 1/4 teaspoon dill weed. Heap over vegetables and bake for 30 minutes.

❦ MACARONI AND CHEESE DELUXE ❦

Puts Kraft's to shame!

Serves 6 to 8.

- 1 8-ounce package elbow macaroni
- 2 cups cream-style cottage cheese
- 1 8-ounce carton sour cream
- 1 egg slightly beaten
- Dash of pepper
- 3/4 teaspoon salt
- 2 cups (8-ounces) shredded sharp Cheddar cheese
- Paprika

Preheat oven to 350°F.

Cook macaroni according to package directions; drain. Rinse macaroni and set aside. Combine next 6 ingredients; add macaroni and stir well. Spoon mixture into a lightly *greased* 2-quart casserole. Sprinkle with paprika and bake for 45 minutes.

🦌 RICE PILAF 🦌

Serves 4.

- 1 tablespoon butter or margarine
- 1 cup long-grain rice
- 1/2 cup finely chopped onion
- 1/4 teaspoon ground cinnamon
- 1/8 teaspoon ground pepper
- 2 cups boiling water
- 1/2 cup chopped parsley

In medium-sized saucepan over medium heat, melt butter. Add rice and onion, cook 2 minutes or until rice is opaque, stirring constantly. Stir in cinnamon and pepper; add boiling water. Cover and reduce heat to low and simmer 20 minutes or until water is absorbed and rice is tender. Just before serving, stir in parsley.

❦ SPANISH RICE ❦

This recipe was originally on the back of a box of rice. It is now a "Southern" classic. The Spaniards have probably never heard of it, so I don't know why it is called Spanish rice.

Serves 6.

- 3 tablespoons bacon fat, divided
- 1 cup uncooked rice (NOT instant or converted)
- 3/4 cup chopped onion
- 1/2 cup chopped green pepper
- 1/2 cup chopped celery
- 1 16-ounce can stewed tomatoes
- 1 cup water
- 1 1/2 teaspoons salt
- 1 teaspoon chili powder

Heat 2 tablespoons of the bacon fat in a large skillet. Add the rice. Cook, stirring frequently, until rice is lightly browned.

Add remaining tablespoon of bacon fat. Stir in onion, green pepper and celery; saute until tender, about 3 minutes.

Stir in tomatoes, water, salt and chili powder. Bring to boiling; lower heat; cover and simmer 20 minutes or until rice is tender. If rice is not then sufficiently tender, add 1/4 cup (or less) more water, cover and continue cooking until tender.

🦌 TURMERIC RICE PILAF 🦌

This makes a delicious accompaniment to any meat or poultry entree.

Serves 4.

- 1/3 cup sliced green onion
- 2 tablespoons butter or margarine
- 1 cup long grain rice
- 1 3/4 cups water
- 1 1/2 teaspoons instant beef bouillon granules
- 1/4 teaspoon salt
- 1/4 to 1/2 teaspoon ground turmeric
- 1/2 cup light raisins, optional

In a large saucepan cook onion in butter or margarine until tender, but not brown. Add rice; cook and stir over low heat until rice is golden. Add water, beef bouillon granules, salt and turmeric; heat to boiling. Reduce heat; cover and simmer 15 minutes. Remove from heat and stir gently. Add raisins if desired. Serve hot.

❧ CHEESY POTATO BAKE ❧

Serves 6.

- 6 medium potatoes, scrubbed
- 1 cup shredded mild Cheddar cheese
- 1/2 cup milk
- 2 tablespoons butter
- 1 8-ounce carton sour cream
- 1/4 cup chopped onion
- 1 teaspoon salt
- 1/4 teaspoon pepper
- Butter
- Paprika

Preheat oven to 350°F.

Cook potatoes in jackets in salted boiling water about 30 minutes or until tender. Chill. Peel and grate potatoes. Combine cheese, milk and 2 tablespoons butter in small saucepan; cook over low heat until butter and cheese melt, stirring occasionally. Remove from heat; stir in sour cream, onion, salt and pepper. Fold cheese mixture into potatoes.

Pour into a *greased* 2-quart casserole; dot with butter and sprinkle with paprika. Bake for 45 minutes.

Side Dishes

🦌 HASH BROWN CHEESE BAKE 🦌

Similar to the Cheesy Potato Bake, but different. This serves a crowd.

Serves 12 to 15.

- 2 pounds frozen shredded hash brown potatoes, thawed
- 2 $10^{3/4}$ cans potato soup, undiluted
- 2 8-ounce cartons commercial sour cream
- 2 cups (8 ounces) grated sharp Cheddar cheese
- 1 cup grated Parmesan cheese

Preheat oven to 350°F.

Combine all ingredients, stirring well. Spoon into a *greased* 13x9x2-inch baking pan. Bake for 40 minutes.

❦ MARNIE'S GREAT POTATOES ❦

This again is similar to Cheesy Potato Casserole and to Hash Brown Cheese Bake, but they are all a little different and all are good.

Serves 12 to 15

- 2 pounds frozen hash browns, thawed ½ hour
- 1 cup diced onion
- 1 stick butter (¼ pound)
- 1 can cream of chicken soup
- 1 pint sour cream
- 2 cups (8 ounces) grated sharp Cheddar cheese
- Salt and pepper to taste
- 1 cup crushed potato chips

Preheat oven to 350°F.

Melt butter and saute onions in butter until translucent. Mix with remaining ingredients, except potato chips and mix well. Pour into 9x12 casserole and sprinkle with potato chips. Bake for 1 hour.

❦ POTATO PANCAKES ❦

These are made in a blender and are so easy! They are especially good with any type of barbecued meat.

Serves 6 to 8.

Place in blender:

    3 eggs

Start blender and slice in:

    5 or 6 medium potatoes, pared
    3 slices onion
    2 large sprigs parsley (optional)

Blend until all vegetables are cut fine, then add:

    1/3 cup flour
    1/4 teaspoon baking powder
    1 1/2 teaspoons salt

Blend just to mix. In skillet, heat bacon drippings. (If you do not save bacon drippings, fry a slice or two of bacon and use those drippings.)* Drop potato mixture from large ladle into hot fat. Brown on each side and remove to paper towel lined pan and keep warm while cooking remainder of pancakes.

*The flavor of the bacon drippings adds so much to the flavor of these pancakes. I would not recommend using any other fat.

🦃 PAN-ROASTED POTATOES 🦃

These are crusty and deep brown on the outside and soft and moist on the inside - just as it says in the recipe.

Serves 4.

    10 to 12 small red potatoes, peeled
    3 tablespoons butter
    1 tablespoon vegetable oil
    3/4 teaspoon salt
    1/4 teaspoon pepper

In a skillet large enough to hold the potatoes loosely in a single layer, melt the butter and heat the oil. Add the potatoes, turning them to coat with the butter and oil. Cover tightly and cook the potatoes over low heat, turning as they brown, for 40 to 45 minutes. When done, the potatoes should be crusty and deep brown on the outside and soft and moist on the inside. Sprinkle with salt and pepper.

🦃 NEW POTATOES AND PEAS 🦃

Serves 4 to 6.

    8 to 10 new, small red potatoes
    1 pound fresh or one 10-ounce package of frozen small green peas
    2 tablespoons butter or margarine
    Salt to taste

Scrub potatoes well, but do not peel. Slice into 1/4-inch slices. Barely cover with water and cook 10 minutes. Drain most of water off, add peas and butter. Cover and cook until potatoes and peas are tender. Add more water, sparingly, if needed. Salt to taste.

🦌 STUFFED POTATOES 🦌

These are for special occasions or company fare. I freeze the ones leftover (if there are any) by wrapping them individually in foil. Thaw and bake as if freshly made. Actually they are not quite as good after being frozen, but still make a great side dish.

Serves 6.

Preheat oven to 400°F.

6 very large Idaho potatoes, well scrubbed

Grease potatoes or wrap individually in foil and bake for 1 hour or until soft.

3 strips of bacon, fried crisp drained and crumbled

Cut potatoes in half lengthwise. Spoon out centers while hot, saving skins and put in mixing bowl.

1 teaspoon salt
1 tablespoon chopped, dried chives
4 ounces butter (1 stick)
3 1/2 tablespoons grated Parmesan cheese
1/2 teaspoon black pepper
1/8 teaspoon Ac'cent
3 to 4 tablespoons sour cream
Light cream or milk, if needed
Paprika

Combine salt, chives, bacon, butter, Parmesan cheese, pepper, Ac'cent and sour cream with spooned out centers of potatoes. Mix with electric mixer for 3 minutes at medium speed, adding more sour cream and light cream or milk to get right consistency (should be thicker than mashed potatoes, but not quite so creamy). Spoon into potato skins; sprinkle lightly with paprika. Brown in hot oven for 5 minutes.

BREADS, MUFFINS AND SUCH

There are no complicated recipes here. I've had only marginal success with yeast breads and besides, the bakeries do an excellent job.

❦ CHIVE AND BLACK PEPPER CORN BREAD ❦

This is a very flavorful bread and is excellent with soups.

Makes 9 squares.

- 3/4 cup yellow cornmeal
- 3/4 cup all-purpose flour
- 1 tablespoon sugar
- 1 1/2 teaspoons cream of tartar
- 3/4 teaspoon baking soda
- 1/2 teaspoon coarsely ground black pepper
- 1/2 teaspoon salt
- 1 cup sour cream
- 1/4 cup snipped fresh chives or 1 tablespoon dried
- 3 tablespoons unsalted butter, melted
- 2 tablespoons milk
- 1 egg, beaten to blend

Preheat oven to 425 °F.

Butter an 8-inch square baking dish. Mix first seven ingredients (or all the dry ingredients) in large bowl. Whisk remaining ingredients in another bowl to blend. Make a well in center of dry ingredients. Add sour cream mixture and stir just until blended.

Spoon batter into prepared dish. Bake until corn bread is golden brown and begins to pull away from sides of pan, about 20 minutes. Cool slightly. Cut into squares. Serve warm or at room temperature.

❦ CORNY CORN BREAD ❦

Serves 4 to 6.

      1 cup yellow cornmeal
      1 tablespoon baking powder
      1 cup sour cream
      1 cup canned cream-style corn
     1/2 cup corn oil
      2 large eggs, beaten lightly
   1 1/2 teaspoons salt

Preheat oven to 400°F.

Generously butter a 12x9x2-inch baking pan.

In a medium sized mixing bowl, combine cornmeal and baking powder. Stir in sour cream, corn, oil, eggs and salt. Mix well and pour into buttered baking pan. Bake for 25 to 30 minutes or until the top is golden. Serve the corn bread hot.

🌽 SOUTHERN CORN BREAD 🌽

This should be baked in a well-seasoned iron skillet or corn stick pans. If you don't have an iron skillet, you can use any good baking pan.

Serves 4 to 6.

- 2 eggs
- 2 cups buttermilk
- 2 cups cornmeal
- 1 teaspoon baking soda
- 1 teaspoon salt
- 2 teaspoons baking powder
- 2 tablespoons bacon drippings

Preheat oven to 450°F.

If iron skillet or iron corn stick pans are used, grease generously with bacon drippings and place in oven when it is turned on; they should be smoking hot. If using any other pan, simply grease it.

Beat eggs in medium bowl; add buttermilk. Set aside.

Combine dry ingredients; stir into egg mixture. Stir in melted bacon drippings from skillet. Pour into prepared pan. Bake for 25 minutes if using skillet or 15 to 20 minutes for corn sticks or muffins.

🍳 GOLDEN CORN BREAD 🍳

This may be baked in muffin tins or corn stick pans, but remember to reduce cooking time by about 5 minutes.

Serves 4 to 6.

- 1 cup yellow cornmeal
- 1 cup all-purpose flour
- 1 tablespoon sugar
- 4 teaspoons baking powder
- 1/2 teaspoon salt
- 1 cup milk
- 1 egg
- Bacon fat or shortening

Preheat oven to 425°F.

Generously grease an 8-inch square pan (muffin tins or cornstick pans). Place pan in preheated oven while mixing batter.

Combine cornmeal, flour, sugar, baking powder and salt. Add milk and egg and beat until fairly smooth, about 1 minute. Pour in melted fat from pan and mix well. Turn mixture into hot pan and bake 20 to 25 minutes.

❦ HUSH PUPPIES ❦

This recipe came from the now defunct Rio Vista Restaurants in Atlanta. They served all the catfish and hush puppies you could eat for a small price. They must have gone broke because of families like mine taking advantage of the offer.

An absolute must with fried fish.

Serves 6.

- 1 3/4 cups yellow cornmeal
- 1/3 cup all-purpose flour
- 3 teaspoons baking powder
- 1 teaspoon salt
- 1/2 cup diced or grated onion
- 1 egg, beaten
- 1/2 cup plus 1 tablespoon buttermilk
- 1/2 cup catsup
- Fat for frying

Combine cornmeal, flour, baking powder, salt and onion. Add egg, buttermilk and catsup. Beat well until blended. Batter should be thick enough to drop in 1 to 1 1/2-inch balls from spoon.

Have fat heated - use enough to cover hush puppies. To drop batter into hot fat, dip spoon first in hot fat, then into batter. Fry 6 to 8 hush puppies at a time until rich brown on all sides.

Breads, Muffins and Such

❦ BUTTERMILK BISCUITS ❦

Never once did I say this was a health-wise cookbook! It is meant only for those who enjoy good food and, even if only occasionally, want to indulge in forbidden food - like using lard to make biscuits.

Makes approximately 30 biscuits.

- 1/2 cup lard
- 1/2 teaspoon salt
- 3 teaspoons baking powder
- 3 cups flour
- 1/2 teaspoon baking soda
- 1 1/4 cups buttermilk

Preheat oven to 425°F.

Cut lard into mixture of dry ingredients using pastry blender or two knives. Slowly add buttermilk. Mix well (but do not knead). Roll onto floured board and cut with biscuit cutter. Bake for about 15 minutes.

❦ SOUTHERN BISCUITS ❦
My Version

Makes approximately 24 biscuits.

- 2 cups self-rising flour
- 1/3 cup Crisco shortening
- 1 cup minus 2 tablespoons buttermilk

Preheat oven to 450°F.

Cut shortening into flour using pastry blender or two knives. Add milk, mix well. Roll out to about 1/2 inch thick. Cut out biscuits with a biscuit cutter. Place on a *greased* cookie sheet. Bake for 12 to 15 minutes.

❦ DILLY CHEESE BREAD ❦

Makes a 9x5-inch loaf.

- 3 cups Bisquick baking mix
- 1 1/2 cups grated sharp Cheddar cheese
- 1 tablespoon sugar
- 1 1/4 cups milk
- 1 egg, lightly beaten
- 1 tablespoon vegetable oil
- 1/2 teaspoon dried dillweed
- 1/2 teaspoon dry mustard

Preheat oven to 350°F.

Generously grease 9x5-inch loaf pan or 6-cup bundt pan.

Combine biscuit mix, cheese and sugar in large bowl. Combine remaining ingredients in second bowl and mix well. Stir into dry mixture, blending thoroughly, then beat slightly to remove lumps. Turn into pan and bake until golden, about 45 to 50 minutes.

🌿 GARLIC BREAD 🌿

Excellent, easy and it looks as though you've spent hours making homemade bread.

- 1 pound loaf frozen bread dough
- 1/4 cup (1/2 stick) unsalted butter
- 1 tablespoon beaten egg
- 1 teaspoon garlic salt
- 1 tablespoon or more finely chopped fresh parsley

Thaw bread just until it can be sliced, about 30 to 45 minutes. Cut into 15 pieces.

Melt butter in small saucepan over low heat. Remove from heat and stir in egg, garlic salt and parsley. Roll bread pieces into balls. Dip each ball into butter mixture, coating completely. Arrange in single layer in BUTTERED 9x5-inch loaf pan. Let rise in warm, draft-free area until dough is doubled in size, about 2½ hours.

Preheat oven to 350°F.

Bake until top is golden brown, about 25 minutes. Let cool slightly before serving.

🍂 PARMESAN PASTRY TWISTS 🍂

During one of those interminable waits in a doctor's office, I found this in an old, old magazine. Yes, I did ask permission before taking the recipe.

These are excellent with soups and salads, or use them instead of garlic bread.

Makes 2 dozen.

- 1 10-ounce package patty shells, thawed
- 1 slightly beaten egg white
- 1/4 cup grated Parmesan cheese
- 2 teaspoons snipped chives

Preheat oven to 425°F.

On a lightly floured surface, roll patty shells slightly to flatten. Place pieces, overlapping slightly, to form a rectangle. Press all edges together to seal. Roll pastry to 12x8-inch rectangle (dough should be 1/8 to 1/4 inch thick). Brush lightly with egg white. Sprinkle cheese and chives over dough. Cut rectangle in half lengthwise. Cut each half crosswise into 12 sticks. Twist ends of sticks several times. Place on an *ungreased* baking sheet. Bake for 8 to 10 minutes.

🐿 BANANA WALNUT MUFFINS 🐿

Makes 12 muffins.

- 6 tablespoons Crisco shortening, melted and cooled
- 1/2 cup sugar
- 1 large egg, beaten slightly
- 1 teaspoon salt
- 1 teaspoon vanilla
- 1 1/2 cups all-purpose flour
- 1 teaspoon baking soda
- 1 teaspoon double-acting baking powder
- 1 cup mashed ripe bananas
- 1/2 cup chopped walnuts

Preheat oven to 350°F.

Butter muffin tins. In a large bowl combine shortening, sugar, egg, salt and vanilla.

In another bowl, sift together flour, soda and baking powder. Add dry ingredients to the shortening mixture and stir the batter until it is just combined (the batter will be lumpy). Fold in bananas and walnuts. Spoon the mixture into prepared muffin tins, filling two-thirds full. Bake the muffins for 15 to 20 minutes or until they are golden.

🦌 OAT 'N ORANGE MUFFINS 🦌

These are a delicious muffin for the health-wise. You can pretend you are being "bad" as you eat them.

Makes 18 muffins.

- 1 cup oat bran
- 1 cup buttermilk
- 1/2 cup raisins
- 1/4 cup orange juice
- 1 teaspoon grated orange rind (zest)
- 1 egg, slightly beaten
- 1/2 cup honey
- 1/4 cup vegetable oil
- 1 cup flour
- 1 1/2 teaspoons baking powder
- 1/2 teaspoon baking soda
- 1/2 teaspoon salt

Preheat oven to 375°F.

Line 18 muffin tins with paper muffin cups or grease lightly.

Combine oat bran, buttermilk, raisins, orange juice and zest. Let sit for 30 minutes.

Mix egg, honey and oil. Add to oat bran mixture and stir well. Sift together flour, baking powder, soda and salt. Add to oat, bran and egg mixture and stir just until mixed.

Fill cups two-thirds full. Bake for 20 to 22 minutes. Remove muffins from tin and cool on rack.

🦃 PUMPKIN MUFFINS 🦃

Makes 12 muffins.

- 1 large egg
- 1/2 cup milk
- 1/2 cup canned pumpkin
- 1/2 cup chopped pecans
- 1/4 cup vegetable oil
- 2 teaspoons grated orange rind
- 1 1/2 cups all-purpose flour
- 1/2 cup sugar
- 2 teaspoons baking powder
- 1/2 teaspoon salt
- 1/2 teaspoon nutmeg
- 12 sugar cubes
- 1/2 cup orange juice

Preheat oven to 375°F.

In a large bowl, beat the egg; add milk, pumpkin, pecans, vegetable oil and orange rind. Combine the mixture well.

In another bowl, combine flour, sugar, baking powder, salt and nutmeg. Add the mixture to the pumpkin mixture and stir the batter until it is just combined. (The batter should be lumpy.) Spoon batter into buttered 1/3-cup muffin tins, filling them two-thirds full. In a small bowl dip 12 sugar cubes into 1/2 cup orange juice and press 1 cube into the center of each muffin. Bake the muffins for 20 to 25 minutes or until they are golden.

❦ BLUEBERRY MUFFINS ❦

Makes 12 muffins.

- 1 cup fresh blueberries
- 2 cups flour
- 1/3 cup sugar
- 1 tablespoon baking powder
- 1 teaspoon salt
- 1 egg, well beaten
- 1 cup milk
- 1/4 cup butter, melted

Preheat oven to 425°F.

Grease 12 medium-sized muffin pans.

Wash berries, discarding any bad ones. Spread on paper toweling to drain. Dry well. Reserve.

Combine flour, sugar, baking powder and salt in medium bowl. Combine egg, milk and melted butter in small bowl; add all at once to dry ingredients; stir quickly and lightly just until liquid is absorbed (batter will be lumpy).

Gently fold in blueberries.

Spoon into prepared muffin pans, filling two-thirds full. Sprinkle with topping (optional). Bake for 20 minutes or until golden brown. Remove from pan at once. Serve hot.

TOPPING:

1 tablespoon sugar and 1 teaspoon grated lemon rind, combined.

🦌 CRANBERRY BREAD 🦌

Makes 1 loaf.

- 1 tablespoon all-purpose flour
- 1½ cups fresh or frozen cranberries, thawed if frozen, coarsely chopped
- ½ cup chopped walnuts
- 2 cups all purpose flour
- 1½ teaspoons baking powder
- ½ teaspoon salt
- 1 cup sugar
- ¼ cup Crisco shortening
- 1 egg, slightly beaten
- ¾ cup orange juice
- 1 tablespoon grated orange rind

Preheat oven to 350°F.

Grease 9x5x3-inch loaf pan.

Sprinkle the 1 tablespoon flour over the cranberries and nuts on wax paper; toss to coat. Reserve.

Sift together the 2 cups flour, baking powder and salt into large bowl; stir in the sugar.

Cut shortening into flour mixture with pastry blender until crumbly. Beat egg with the orange juice in a small bowl. Stir into the flour mixture just until the dry ingredients are moistened. Stir in cranberry-nut mixture and orange rind. Spoon into prepared loaf pan.

Bake for 1 hour and 5 minutes or until wooden toothpick inserted in center comes out clean. Turn out onto wire rack to cool. This bread slices better the next day.

🦌 PUMPKIN BREAD 🦌

This makes one loaf but I always double it and make two loaves. That solves the problem of what to do with the leftover pumpkin. The second loaf can be frozen.

- 2 eggs
- 1½ cups sugar
- 1 cup canned pumpkin
- ½ cup salad oil
- 1⅔ cups flour
- ¼ teaspoon baking powder
- 1 teaspoon baking soda
- ½ teaspoon nutmeg
- ½ teaspoon cinnamon
- ½ cup water

Preheat oven to 325°F.

Grease a 9x5-inch loaf pan. Line with brown paper (use a grocery bag, cut to size) and grease paper.

Mix all ingredients together. Fill prepared pan two-thirds full and bake approximately 1 hour and 15 minutes. Check for doneness by inserting a wooden toothpick in the center. If done, the toothpick will come out clean. Remove paper before storing.

🎀 BANANA-NUT BREAD 🎀

Makes 1 loaf.

- 2 2/3 cups all-purpose flour
- 3 teaspoons baking powder
- 1 teaspoon salt
- 1/4 teaspoon baking soda
- 1/2 cup (1 stick) butter, softened
- 1 cup sugar
- 3 eggs
- 2 ripe bananas, mashed
- 3/4 cup chopped walnuts
- 2 teaspoons grated orange rind (optional)

Preheat oven to 325°F.

Grease a 9x5x3-inch loaf pan; line bottom with waxed paper; grease paper.

Combine flour, baking powder, salt and baking soda. Set aside.

Cream butter with sugar until fluffy in a large bowl. Beat in eggs, one at a time, until fluffy again.

Stir in flour mixture, alternately with mashed bananas; fold in nuts and orange rind. Pour into prepared pan. Bake for 1 hour and 20 minutes. Test for doneness by inserting a wooden toothpick in center. When toothpick comes out clean, it is done. You may need to bake it longer than suggested.

Wrap and store overnight for easier slicing. (Remove waxed paper before storing.)

DESSERTS

Really good dessert recipes are so easy to find. Any good recipe book will have dozens. The ones included here are some of my favorites and some that I don't think you will find in another cookbook.

🦌 GRASSHOPPER PIE 🦌

This is a recipe that was very popular a few years ago. It is still an excellent dessert. It is very easy to make.

CRUST:

- 1 1/2 cups chocolate wafer crumbs*
- 1/3 to 1/2 cup melted butter

In a small bowl, combine chocolate crumbs and butter; blend well. Pat crumbs onto bottom and sides of 9-inch pie plate. Chill.

FILLING:

- 48 marshmallows
- 1 1/3 cups milk
- 2 cups whipping cream
- 1/2 cup green creme de menthe
- 1/4 cup creme de cacao
- 1/4 cup whipping cream, whipped, for garnish
- 1/2 cup strawberries, for garnish

Combine marshmallows and milk in a 3-quart saucepan; cook over low heat, stirring constantly, until marshmallows are melted. Cool to room temperature. Whip the two cups whipping cream until soft peaks form in a chilled large bowl. Fold in creme de menthe and creme de cacao. If necessary, beat marshmallow mixture to make it smooth. Fold into the whipped cream. Gently pour into the pie shell. Freeze overnight before serving. Garnish with whipped cream and strawberries.

*Crushed Oreos, with the white filling removed, work well.

❧ COCONUT CREAM PIE ❧

Luscious!!! Absolutely calorie free! Now if you believe that... Once I would have said to make your own pie crust, but now there are so many good ones on the market, that unless you are a purist, use a ready made one.

    1/4 cup flour
    1/2 cup sugar
    1/4 teaspoon salt
1 1/2 cups scalded milk*
      3 eggs, separated (save whites for meringue)
      2 tablespoons butter
    1/2 teaspoon vanilla
    1/3 cup sugar
      1 cup moist, shredded coconut
        Baked 9-inch pie shell

Preheat oven to 350°F.

Mix flour, 1/2 cup sugar and salt in top of double boiler; add 3/4 cup of the scalded milk and stir vigorously until well blended. Add remaining hot milk and cook over direct heat until thick and smooth, stirring constantly. Beat egg yolks well, stir a little of the hot mixture** into the egg yolks, then pour into the flour-mixture in double boiler; cook over boiling water for 2 minutes, stirring constantly. Remove from heat and stir in butter and vanilla. Fold in 2/3 cup coconut. Set aside.

Beat egg whites until stiff and gradually beat in 1/3 cup of sugar until very thick and smooth. Fold about 1/3 cup of the meringue into the hot filling. Pour filling into pie shell. Pile remaining meringue over filling, being sure to touch the edges of the crust all around. Sprinkle with the remaining 1/3 cup coconut. Bake for 12 to 15 minutes or until golden brown. Cool on cake rack before cutting.

*To scald milk, heat just until it begins to bubble around the sides of pan. Do not boil.

**This prevents the eggs from curdling as they would if you just poured them into the hot filling.

Desserts

🦌 CHOCOLATE LUSCIOUS PIE 🦌

The name is very appropriate!!!

- 1½ cups graham cracker crumbs
- ½ cup finely chopped pecans
- ⅓ cup brown sugar
- ½ cup melted butter

Preheat oven to 300°F.

Butter a 10-inch pie pan. Combine all crust ingredients and pack firmly onto bottom and sides of pie pan. Bake for 5 minutes. Cool.

FILLING:

- 1¼ cups milk
- ⅓ cup sugar
- 2 egg yolks, beaten lightly
- 1 envelope Knox plain gelatin, softened in ¼ cup milk
- 1 cup whipping cream, whipped
- 2 egg whites, beaten until stiff
- 1 square semisweet chocolate, shaved (cut with a vegetable peeler)
- 1 teaspoon vanilla
- ½ cup chocolate chips
- ⅓ cup water
- 1 tablespoon butter

Heat milk with ⅓ cup sugar. Add a little of the milk mixture to the egg yolks and then put egg yolks into milk mixture, stirring constantly. Add gelatin mixture. Fold in the whipped cream and the beaten egg whites. Add shaved chocolate. Stir in vanilla. Pour into crust, chill until set.

Heat chocolate chips in ⅓ cup water and butter, stirring to make a smooth sauce. Drizzle over the top of the pie. Serve chilled and with additional whipped cream, if desired.

🌶 LEMON MERINGUE PIE 🌶

A perpetual favorite!

Nine-inch pastry shell, baked and cooled*

FILLING:

- 1/2 to 3/4 teaspoon lemon rind, packed
- 1/3 cup strained lemon juice (juice of 2 medium lemons)
- 1/4 cup cornstarch plus 2 tablespoons all-purpose flour
- 1 1/3 cups sugar
- 1/4 teaspoon salt
- 1 1/2 cups boiling water
- 3 egg yolks (save egg whites for meringue)
- 2 tablespoons firm butter

MERINGUE:

- Dash of salt
- 3 egg whites
- 1/3 cup sugar
- 1 teaspoon sugar for sprinkling on top of meringue (if desired)

Preheat oven to 350°F.

Blend cornstarch, flour, sugar and salt in a 3-quart saucepan. Stir in boiling water. Place over direct heat, cook and stir constantly until thick and clear, about 3 minutes. Beat egg yolks, then quickly stir in about 1/3 cup of hot mixture to prevent curdling Pour egg mixture into saucepan and cook, stirring constantly, for about 2 minutes. Remove from heat, stir in butter, then the rind, then the lemon juice gradually in small portions, mixing well after each addition. Pour into cooled pie shell.

MEANWHILE MAKE MERINGUE: Add salt to egg whites and beat until just stiff, then gradually beat in $1/3$ cup sugar until meringue is stiff and shiny. Spread lightly over pie so it touches crust all around; swirl or spread smooth. Sprinkle with the teaspoon of sugar, if desired.

Bake for 12 to 15 minutes or until golden brown. Remove to cake rack out of draft, to cool before cutting.

*Any good pie shell recipe will be fine - or if you prefer, use a frozen or other ready-made crust.

🍒 MILE-HIGH RASPBERRY PIE 🍒

A huge success!

- 1 10-inch pie shell, unbaked
- 1/2 cup slivered almonds
- 1 10-ounce package frozen raspberries, thawed
- 3 egg whites
- 1 tablespoon lemon juice
- 1 cup sugar
- 1 teaspoon almond extract
- 1 cup whipping cream, whipped

Preheat oven to 450°F.

Press almonds into prepared pie shell. Bake until golden brown about 10 to 12 minutes.

Mix in a large bowl, raspberries, egg whites, lemon juice, sugar and almond extract and beat until very stiff. This will splatter like the dickens, so be sure to use a large bowl. Fold in whipped cream. Spoon into pie shell and freeze at least 5 hours. Remove from freezer 15 minutes before serving.

🎔 CHOCOLATE PIE 🎔

This is a basic kind of dessert, but I include it because it is so good.

- 2 squares unsweetened chocolate
- 2 tablespoons butter
- 1/3 cup flour
- 1 cup sugar
- 1/4 teaspoon salt
- 2 1/2 cups milk, scalded*
- 3 eggs, separated
- 3/4 teaspoon vanilla
- 1/3 cup sugar
- Baked 9-inch pie shell**

Preheat oven to 350°F.

Melt chocolate and butter in top of double boiler. Mix flour, sugar and salt and stir into chocolate. Add 1 cup hot milk and stir until smooth. Add remaining milk and cook until thickened.

Beat egg yolks slightly. Mix a little hot mixture into beaten egg yolks, then put egg mixture into chocolate mixture. (This step prevents egg yolks from curdling when put in the hot mixture.) Cook a minute or so. Remove from heat and add vanilla. Pour into pie shell.

Beat egg whites, slowly adding 1/3 cup sugar, until meringue will hold a stiff peak. Pile over pie filling. Bake 12 to 15 minutes until golden brown.

Cool before slicing.

*To scald milk, heat milk just until it begins to bubble around the edges. Do not boil.

**You can use one of the great ready-made pie shells.

🌿 PECAN PIE 🌿

Pecan pies are so easy to make that some good Southern cooks never use a recipe. Not I. This is the one I use.

- 1 9-inch unbaked pie shell
- 1 cup white corn syrup
- 3/4 cup sugar
- 1/4 teaspoon salt
- 1 teaspoon vanilla
- 1/4 cup melted butter
- 3 eggs, slightly beaten
- 1 cup pecan meats

Preheat oven to 425°F.

Combine syrup, sugar, salt, vanilla and butter. Stir in eggs well, but do not beat. Fold in pecans. Pour into pie shell. Bake for 10 minutes, then reduce heat to moderately slow oven (325°F) and bake 35 to 40 minutes longer or until crust and filling are golden brown. Remove to cake rack and cool.

Serve with whipped cream if desired.

🌰 BLUEBERRY COBBLER 🌰

Serve this with a large scoop of vanilla ice cream.

Serves 8 to 10.

BLUEBERRY FILLING:

    4 cups fresh or frozen blueberries
    5 tablespoons sugar
    3/4 cup orange juice

TOPPING:

    1 cup flour
    1/2 teaspoon baking powder
    1/8 teaspoon salt
    1/2 pound butter, softened
    1 cup sugar
    1 egg
    1/2 teaspoon vanilla extract
    Vanilla ice cream

Preheat oven to 375°F.

FOR THE FILLING: Mix all ingredients in a 9x13-inch baking pan. Set aside.

FOR THE TOPPING: Mix first 3 ingredients in a small bowl. Set aside.

Mix butter and sugar in a large bowl until well blended. Stir in egg and vanilla extract, then stir in flour mixture. Drop this topping by tablespoonfuls on top of the blueberry filling.

TO COOK: Bake until cobbler topping is golden brown and filling is bubbly, 35 to 40 minutes. Spoon a scoop of ice cream atop each serving.

🌣 BLUEBERRY LEMON POUND CAKE 🌣

This is a great pound cake. Toasted and buttered, it makes an excellent breakfast food or snack - or for whenever you feel the urge to indulge.

    1 teaspoon baking powder
  1/4 teaspoon salt
    1 cup plain yogurt
    2 sticks (1 cup) unsalted butter, softened
    2 cups granulated sugar, divided
    6 large eggs, separated and at room temperature
    4 teaspoons grated lemon rind
    2 tablespoons fresh lemon juice
    3 cups cake flour
      Pinch of cream of tartar
 1 1/2 cups blueberries, picked over and tossed with 1 tablespoon flour
    1 tablespoon confectioners' sugar

Preheat oven to 375°F.

Combine flour, baking powder and salt and set aside.

In a large bowl cream the butter, add 1 1/2 cups of the granulated sugar, a little at a time, beating after each addition and beat the mixture until it is light and fluffy. Beat in the egg yolks, one at a time, beating well after each addition. Add the lemon rind and the lemon juice. Stir in the flour mixture alternately with the yogurt.

In a bowl with an electric mixer beat the egg whites with the cream of tartar and a pinch of salt until they hold soft peaks. Beat in gradually, the remaining 1/2 cup granulated sugar. Beat the meringue until it holds stiff peaks. Stir 1/4th of the meringue into the yogurt mixture and fold in the remaining meringue gently but thoroughly. Fold in the blueberries and spoon the batter into a buttered and floured 4-quart tube pan, 4 inches deep and smooth the top.

Bake the cake for 1 hour or until a cake tester inserted halfway between the center and the edges comes out clean.

Let the cake cool in the pan on a rack for 10 minutes, then invert onto a rack and let it cool completely. Sift the confectioners' sugar over the cake and transfer the cake to a platter.

❦ RASPBERRY WALNUT TORTE ❦

When I can't get out of serving dessert to my bridge group, I serve this. It has always been a big hit.

   1¼ cups flour, divided
   ⅓ cup powdered sugar
   ½ cup soft butter
   1 10-ounce package frozen raspberries, thawed
   ¾ cup chopped walnuts
   2 eggs
   1 cup sugar
   ½ teaspoon salt
   ½ teaspoon baking powder
   1 teaspoon vanilla

Preheat oven to 350°F.

Combine 1 cup flour, powdered sugar and butter; blend well. Press into bottom of 13x9-inch pan. Bake for 15 minutes. Cool.

Drain raspberries, reserving liquid for sauce. Spoon berries over crust. Sprinkle with walnuts. Beat eggs with sugar until light and fluffy. Add salt and remaining ¼ cup flour, baking powder and vanilla; blend well and pour over walnuts.

Bake for 30 to 35 minutes. Cool. Cut into squares. Serve with whipped cream or ice cream and sauce.

SAUCE:

- 1/2 cup water
- 2 tablespoons cornstarch
- 1/2 cup sugar
- Raspberry juice
- 1 tablespoon lemon juice

Cook water, cornstarch, sugar and raspberry juice until thickened, stirring constantly. Add lemon juice.

🍎 GOLDEN APPLE TORTE 🍎

This is easy and scrumptious.

- 3 cups flour
- 2 teaspoons baking soda
- 1/2 teaspoon salt
- 2 teaspoons cinnamon
- 1 1/2 cups oil
- 1 1/2 cups sugar
- 2 cups grated Delicious apples
- 1 9-ounce can crushed pineapple
- 1/2 cup chopped walnuts
- 1 1/2 teaspoons vanilla
- 3 eggs
- Lemon glaze (recipe follows)
- 2 tablespoons finely chopped walnuts

Preheat oven to 350°F.

Sift together flour, soda, salt and cinnamon. Combine oil and sugar.

Add half of dry ingredients to oil and sugar, mixing well. Blend in grated apples, pineapple, 1/2 cup walnuts and vanilla. Add remaining dry ingredients. Add eggs, one at a time, beating well after each addition. Turn into a *greased* 3-quart bundt pan. Bake for 1 hour or until toothpick comes out clean when inserted in center of the cake. Cool in pan 15 minutes; turn out on wire rack.

Drizzle with Lemon Glaze and sprinkle with 2 tablespoons chopped walnuts when cool.

LEMON GLAZE:

Combine 1 1/2 cups powered sugar, 3 tablespoons soft butter, 1/2 teaspoon grated lemon peel, 2 teaspoons lemon juice and 1 1/2 tablespoons hot water. Stir until smooth.

🦌 MARTHA'S RICE PUDDING 🦌

A great way to use up left-over rice. PLEASE, please do not use "instant rice". It does not taste like rice, does not cook up like rice and can ruin any dish in which you use rice.

- 2 cups milk or milk and cream
- 1 teaspoon vanilla
- 1 egg, well beaten
- 3/4 cup raisins
- 1 1/2 cups cooked rice
- 1/2 cup sugar
- 1/2 teaspoon nutmeg

Preheat oven to 325°F.

Mix all ingredients together. Place in a buttered 8x8-inch baking dish and bake for 1 hour. Serve with thin or whipped cream.

🍒 BANANA PUDDING 🍒

If you are a Southerner you have probably eaten this and may have the recipe. It was on the package of Nabisco 'Nilla Wafers years ago. It is as good today as then.

Serves 8.

- ¾ cup sugar, divided
- 3 tablespoons flour
- Dash of salt
- 1 egg
- 3 eggs, separated, saving whites for meringue
- 2 cups milk
- ½ teaspoon vanilla
- Nabisco 'Nilla Wafers
- 5 to 6 medium-size, fully ripe bananas, sliced

Preheat oven to 425°F.

Combine ½ cup of sugar, flour and salt in top of a double boiler. Beat in 1 whole egg and 3 egg yolks; stir in milk. Cook over simmering water, stirring constantly, until thickened, about 15 minutes. Remove from heat; stir in vanilla.

Spread a small amount of custard on bottom of a 1½-quart baking dish; cover with a layer of the wafers. Top with a layer of sliced bananas. Pour about ⅓ of the custard over bananas slices. Continue to layer wafers, bananas and custard to make 3 layers of each, ending with custard.

Beat 3 remaining egg whites in a small bowl with electric mixer until foamy white; gradually add remaining ¼ cup sugar and beat until mixture forms stiff peaks. Swirl on top of pudding, covering entire top surface.

Bake for 5 minutes or until meringue is delicately browned. Serve warm or chilled.

❦ CRANBERRY CRISP ❦

Serves 6 to 8.

- 2 cups cranberries (thawed if frozen), picked over
- 3/4 cup sugar, divided
- 1/2 cup coarsely chopped pecans
- 6 tablespoons unsalted butter, melted and cooled, divided
- 1 large egg, beaten lightly
- 1/2 cup all-purpose flour
- 1/2 teaspoon cinnamon
- 1/8 teaspoon grated nutmeg
- Confectioners' sugar for garnish
- Vanilla ice cream as an accompaniment

Preheat oven to 350°F.

Spread the cranberries in a well-buttered, shallow 8-inch round baking dish, (cake pan or pie plate will do fine). In a small bowl combine ¼ cup of sugar, pecans and 2 tablespoons of the melted butter and sprinkle over the cranberries.

Sift flour, cinnamon and nutmeg together. Set aside.

In a bowl beat the egg with the remaining ½ cup sugar until the mixture is combined, stir in the flour mixture and add the remaining butter, 1 tablespoon at a time, beating well after each addition. Pour the batter over the cranberries in an even layer and bake the crisp for 45 minutes. Sift the confectioners' sugar over the dessert and serve the dessert with the ice cream.

🦌 COLONIAL BREAD PUDDING 🦌

We found that this is best when served cold and topped with vanilla ice cream.

Serves 8 to 10.

- 1 cup raisins
- 1 cup bourbon
- 10 to 12 bread slices, cubed
- 2½ cups whipping cream
- 1½ cups sugar
- 2½ cups applesauce
- 6 tablespoons unsalted butter, melted
- ¼ teaspoon salt
- ½ teaspoon grated nutmeg
- 1 teaspoon cinnamon
- 3 large eggs, beaten lightly
- 2 teaspoons vanilla
- 1⅓ cup pecans, chopped

Preheat oven to 350°F.

Soak raisins in bourbon for 1 hour or longer. Drain. Generously butter a 13x9-inch baking dish. Put cubed bread in buttered dish. Combine cream, sugar, applesauce, butter, salt, nutmeg, cinnamon, raisins, eggs, vanilla and pecans. Pour mixture over the bread, stirring slightly to allow the liquid to cover all the bread cubes. Cover with foil and bake for 1 hour or until center is firm - firm, not dry! Cool thoroughly before serving.

❦ REBECCA SAUCE ❦

Serve over fresh fruit for a scrumptious dessert.

Makes 2 cups.

- 1 1/2 cups sour cream
- 1/4 cup firmly packed brown sugar
- 1 tablespoon rum
- 1 tablespoon Irish whiskey
- 1/4 cup raisins

Combine first 4 ingredients in medium bowl and whisk until smooth. Blend in raisins. Cover with plastic wrap and refrigerate at least 2 hours.

CARAMEL BANANAS WITH RUM

Serves 4.

- 2/3 cup packed brown sugar
- 2 tablespoons whipping cream
- 1 tablespoon butter
- 3 tablespoons rum
- 1/2 cup chilled whipping cream
- 1 tablespoon packed brown sugar
- 4 medium bananas
- 1/4 cup sliced almonds, toasted

Cook and stir 2/3 cup brown sugar, 2 tablespoons whipping cream and butter over low heat until sugar is dissolved and mixture is smooth. Remove from heat; stir in rum. Whip remaining cream with 1 tablespoon brown sugar. Top bananas with caramel sauce, whipped cream and almonds.

If you are in a hurry, melt a caramel sauce (commercial) and add rum to the sauce. Use a ready whipped topping instead of whipped cream.

❦ AMBROSIA ❦

"Ambrosia" means the food of the Gods and this comes close. Served with a slice of pound cake, angel food cake or even fruit cake, it makes a great holiday dessert. We like it with no cake at all.

Serves 10.

- 4 large navel oranges
- 1 12-ounce package frozen pineapple*
- 2 tablespoons Cointreau or other orange liqueur
- 4 medium bananas
- 4 tablespoons confectioners' sugar
- 1 3½-ounce can flaked coconut

Peel oranges; remove white membrane. Cut oranges crosswise into ⅛-inch slices.

Drain pineapple, saving syrup. Combine syrup and Cointreau; set aside. Peel bananas. Cut on the diagonal into ⅛-inch slices.

In an attractive serving bowl, layer half the orange slices; sprinkle with 2 tablespoons confectioners' sugar. Layer half the bananas and half the pineapple; sprinkle with half the coconut. Repeat layers of fruit and sugar. Pour syrup mixture over fruit. Sprinkle with remaining coconut.

Refrigerate several hours or until well chilled.

*If you cannot find frozen pineapple, you may use canned.

🦌 OLD TIME FRIED PIES 🦌

These are a great Southern snack time treat, but you don't have to be a Southerner to enjoy them.

Makes 10 pies.

PIE FILLING:

- 1/2 pound dried apples
- 2 1/2 cups cold water
- 1/2 cup sugar, divided
- 2 tablespoons melted butter
- 1/4 teaspoon nutmeg or cloves or 1 teaspoon cinnamon

TO PREPARE DRIED APPLES: Remove any dark spots from apples. Rinse in cold water. Place in 2-quart saucepan, add cold water and soak 3 to 4 hours. Heat to boiling over moderate heat, reduce heat, cover and simmer 15 to 20 minutes or until soft. Stir in 1/4 cup sugar and simmer 5 minutes longer. Cool.

Mix cooked apples, remaining 1/4 cup sugar, butter and spice. Set aside.

PASTRY:

- 2 cups flour
- 1 teaspoon salt
- 1/3 cup Crisco shortening
- 4 to 5 tablespoons ice water
- Oil for frying

Combine pastry ingredients. Roll out to 1/8-inch thick on lightly floured surface. Cut into 5-inch rounds (using the removeable plastic top of a 1-pound coffee can). Put a large spoonful of filling on 1/2 of circle, keeping it 1/2 inch from edge of pastry. Brush edge of pastry with water. Fold pastry over filling, making a half moon. Seal edges by pressing with tines of fork.

Prick top of pies with fork. Heat oil in heavy skillet to 360°F (hot, but not smoking). Slide 4 or 5 pies into hot oil using pancake turner. Fry until golden, turning once.

❦ KAHLUA PARFAIT ❦

This is a good, simple way to finish your dinner party with a flourish. In the last section of this book, BEVERAGES, you will find a recipe for homemade Kahlua. It is much cheaper and as good as the "store bought" kind.

Layer Kahlua and coffee ice cream in a parfait glass, starting and finishing with Kahlua.

You may do this days ahead and keep in the freezer until ready to serve. Be sure to cover the parfait glasses with plastic wrap before putting in the freezer.

COOKIES AND BARS

These recipes have come to me from a multitude of sources. My children loved cookies and now, my grandchildren think my cookie jar should always be full.

❦ RAISIN OATMEAL COOKIES ❦

Makes about 75 cookies.

    3 cups all-purpose flour
    2 cups old-fashioned rolled oats
    2 teaspoons baking soda
    1 teaspoon salt
    2 teaspoons ground cinnamon
    2 sticks (1 cup) unsalted butter, softened
    2 cups sugar
  1 1/2 teaspoons vanilla
    2 large eggs
  1/2 cup unsulfured molasses*
    1 cup sweetened, flaked coconut
    1 cup raisins, soaked in hot water to cover for 30 minutes and drained well

Preheat oven to 350°F.

In a bowl stir together the flour, oats, baking soda, salt and cinnamon. In another bowl, with an electric mixer, cream together the butter and the sugar until the mixture is light and fluffy. Then beat in the vanilla, the eggs, 1 at a time, beating well after each addition and then the molasses. Stir in the flour mixture, the coconut and the raisins. Roll rounded tablespoons of the dough into balls and arrange the balls on a lightly *greased* cookie sheet, 2 inches apart. (They will flatten as they cook.) Bake the cookies in batches in the middle of the oven for 12 to 15 minutes or until they are golden. Transfer them to racks to cool.

*Molasses that have not had sulfur added. It will say unsulfured on the label.

❦ CHERRY SURPRISE BALLS ❦

Easy and delicious.

Makes 6 dozen cookies.

- 1 cup butter, softened
- 1/2 cup confectioners' sugar
- 2 cups flour
- 1 teaspoon vanilla
- 1/2 cup finely chopped walnuts or pecans
- 1 pound candied cherries

Preheat oven to 375°F.

Cream butter and sugar until light and fluffy. Add flour and vanilla. Stir in walnuts. Chill for several hours. Roll enough dough around each cherry to make 3/4-inch balls.

Place on an *ungreased* cookie sheet. Bake for 20 minutes. While still warm, roll in sifted confectioners' sugar.

May be frozen.

🦌 O'HENRY BARS 🦌

Actually these are more of a candy bar.

Makes twenty 2-inch bars.

    2/3 cup butter, softened
    1 cup brown sugar
    1/2 cup light corn syrup
    3 teaspoons vanilla
    4 cups quick cooking oats
    1 6-ounce package chocolate chips
    2/3 cup peanut butter

Preheat oven to 350°F.

Cream butter and sugar; stir in corn syrup, vanilla and oats. Spread into a *greased* 13x9-inch pan. Bake for 15 minutes. Cool.

Melt chocolate chips and peanut butter in heavy saucepan over low heat. Spread this mixture over cooled oatmeal mixture. Let cool completely and cut into bars.

🐿 PECANETTES 🐿

These take some time to prepare, but they are worth it.

Makes 24 Pecanettes.

>   1   3-ounce package cream cheese, softened
> 1/4   pound (1 stick) butter, softened
>   1   cup flour

Mix well and shape into roll about 12 inches long and store in refrigerator.

Mix well together:

> 3/4   cup dark brown sugar
>   1   tablespoon melted butter
> 2/3   cup chopped pecans
>   1   egg, beaten
>   1   teaspoon vanilla
>   **Dash of salt**

Preheat oven to 350°F.

Cut roll of dough into 24 1/2-inch slices and place in an *ungreased* miniature muffin tins, working dough up around sides. Add 1 teaspoon of filling per muffin cup and bake for 25 to 30 minutes. Cool completely before removing.

Recipe doubles easily. May be frozen.

❦ BOURBON BALLS ❦

Your spouse's office crew will love these at Christmas time.

Makes 3 dozen.

- 1 6-ounce package chocolate chips
- 1/2 cup sugar
- 3 tablespoons light corn syrup
- 1/2 cup bourbon
- 2 1/2 cups vanilla wafers, crushed fine
- 1 cup walnuts, finely chopped
- Granulated sugar

Melt chocolate chips over hot water in double boiler. Remove from heat. Stir in sugar and corn syrup. Blend in bourbon.

Combine crushed wafers and nuts. Add chocolate mixture to wafers. Mix well. Shape into 1-inch balls. Roll them in granulated sugar.

Let balls set in covered container for several days to ripen. Will keep for weeks, but do not freeze.

🍒 ORANGE FRUITCAKE BARS 🍒

My penciled notation on this recipe says "excellent" and that says it all.

Makes 100 bars.

- 1 6-ounce can frozen orange juice, thawed and undiluted
- 1/2 cup and 2/3 cup packed brown sugar
- 1 cup raisins
- 1 8-ounce package pitted dates, chopped
- 1 pound mixed candied fruit, finely chopped
- 1/2 cup butter or margarine, softened
- 4 eggs
- 1 cup unsifted flour
- 1/8 teaspoon baking soda
- 1/2 teaspoon cinnamon
- 1/2 teaspoon nutmeg
- 1/4 teaspoon allspice
- 1/4 teaspoon ground cloves
- 1 cup chopped nuts
- Candied cherries, optional

Preheat oven to 300°F.

In medium saucepan combine orange juice and 1/2 cup packed brown sugar. Stir over low heat until mixture comes to boil. Add raisins and dates and bring to boil again. Remove from heat, stir in mixed candied fruit and set aside.

In large bowl, cream butter and 2/3 cup brown sugar. Beat in eggs, one at a time. Blend in flour, baking soda, cinnamon, nutmeg, allspice and cloves. Stir in nuts and fruit mixture. Turn into 2 wax paper-lined 15x10x1-inch baking sheets. Bake for 35 to 40 minutes or until cake tester inserted in center comes out clean. Cool. Cut into 3x1-inch bars. Garnish with candied cherries if desired.

❦ DATE FILLED SQUARES ❦

There are thousands of versions of this cookie bar, but this is the best I've found.

   About 40 dates, cut up
- 1 cup sugar
- 1 cup water

Boil together until thick and smooth. Add ½ teaspoon vanilla and allow to cool.

BATTER:

- 1½ cups flour
- ½ teaspoon soda
- ½ teaspoon salt
- 1 cup brown sugar
- 1½ cups rolled oats
- 1 cup melted butter
- 1 cup chopped walnuts

Preheat oven to 350°F.

Mix flour, soda, salt, sugar and oats together. Add nuts and melted butter. Work with hands thoroughly. Pat ½ mixture into a shallow *greased* 12x8-inch pan. Spread date filling over it. Then pat balance of oatmeal mixture over date filling. Pat down firmly.

Bake for 45 minutes.

Cool and cut into squares. Roll in confectioners' sugar, if desired.

🌱 OATMEAL COOKIES 🌱

I found this recipe in a little mission magazine about 35 years ago. The caption said they were to oatmeal cookies what the Cadillac was to the T-Model. I promise they will be the best oatmeal cookies you've ever tasted.

1. Cream together:

    1 cup Crisco shortening
    1/2 cup brown sugar
    1 cup white sugar

2. Add one beaten egg.

3. Sift together:

    1 1/2 cups flour
    1 teaspoon cinnamon
    1 teaspoon soda

4. Add to first mixture.

5. Then add:

    1 1/2 cups quick rolled oats
    3/4 cup crushed walnuts
    1 teaspoon vanilla

Preheat oven to 350°F.

You will need to put your spoon aside and mix this with your hands. The mixture will be much dryer than you would expect.

Put walnut size pieces on a *greased* cookie sheet. Butter the bottom of a small glass, dip in granulated sugar and flatten the little pieces. Just keep doing this - you do not need to re-butter the glass bottom, just re-sugar it each time. Bake for 10 minutes.

🍒 PINEAPPLE COOKIES 🍒

Different, but very good. They are a moist cookie, so don't store them with the crisp ones.

SIFT TOGETHER:

- 2 cups flour
- 1/4 teaspoon soda
- 1 1/2 teaspoons baking powder
- 1/4 teaspoon salt

MIX TOGETHER:

- 1/2 cup Crisco shortening
- 1 well beaten egg
- 1 cup brown sugar, packed
- 1 teaspoon vanilla
- 1 small can crushed pineapple, drained with juice reserved

Preheat oven to 350°F.

Add dry ingredients in parts to pineapple mixture, mix well and drop from teaspoon onto a *greased* cookie sheet. Bake 10 to 12 minutes.

GLAZE:

- 2 1/2 tablespoons pineapple juice
- 1 1/2 cups confectioners' sugar

Mix together well and put glaze on cookies while they are still hot.

🍒 CARAMEL BROWNIES 🍒

This recipe makes lots and lots of brownies. I do not know how you would cut it down, but fortunately they freeze very well.

- 1 two-layer German chocolate cake mix
- 3/4 cup butter or margarine, melted
- 2/3 cup evaporated milk, divided
- 1 cup chopped walnuts or pecans
- 1 6-ounce package chocolate chips
- 14 ounces light caramel candies (the type that are individually wrapped)

Preheat oven to 350°F.

Combine cake mix, butter and 1/3 cup evaporated milk. Mix well. Press 1/2 mixture into an *ungreased* 13x9-inch pan. Bake for 5 minutes.

Sprinkle nuts and chocolate chips over cake crust. Melt caramel candies with remaining 1/3 cup milk in saucepan over low heat until smooth. Stir frequently. Pour over nuts and chips then top with remaining 1/2 cake mixture. Press gently. Bake for 20 minutes. Cool slightly. Cut into small squares.

❦ PEANUT BLOSSOMS ❦

Bound to be a favorite with the younger set - from three to ninety.

Makes 4 dozen cookies.

- 1 3/4 cups all-purpose flour
- 1 teaspoon baking soda
- 1/2 teaspoon salt
- 1/2 cup sugar
- 1/2 cup packed light brown sugar
- 1/2 cup shortening
- 1/2 cup creamy peanut butter
- 1 egg
- 2 tablespoons milk
- 1 teaspoon vanilla
- 48 chocolate kisses, unwrapped

Preheat oven to 375°F.

In large mixer bowl, stir flour, soda and salt together. Add remaining ingredients except candy and mix at medium speed of electric mixer until well combined, scraping sides of bowl occasionally. Chill dough 30 minutes.

Roll small amount of dough into 1-inch balls. Place on an *ungreased* cookie sheet and bake for 12 minutes or until light brown. Remove from oven and immediately press a chocolate kiss into center of each cookie. (The cookie cracks around the edges.)

🦌 BANANA DROP COOKIES 🦌

Another moist cookie. Do not store with crisp ones.

- 2 cups all-purpose flour
- 1 1/2 teaspoons baking powder
- 1/2 teaspoon ground cinnamon
- 1/4 teaspoon baking soda
- 1/4 teaspoon salt
- 1/4 teaspoon ground cloves
- 1/2 cup butter or margarine, softened
- 1 cup sugar
- 2 eggs
- 1/2 teaspoon vanilla
- 2 medium bananas, mashed (about 1 cup)
- 1/2 cup chopped walnuts
- Banana Butter Frosting (recipe follows)

Preheat oven to 375°F.

Mix together flour, baking powder, cinnamon, baking soda, salt and cloves thoroughly. Set aside.

In mixer bowl beat butter or margarine with electric mixer on medium speed for 30 seconds. Add sugar and beat until fluffy. Add eggs and vanilla; beat well.

Add dry ingredients and mashed bananas alternately to the beaten mixture and beat until well blended. Stir in the chopped walnuts.

Drop from a teaspoon 2 inches apart onto a *greased* cookie sheet. Bake for 10 to 12 minutes or until done. Immediately remove from cookie sheet; cool on wire rack. Frost with Banana Butter Frosting.

BANANA BUTTER FROSTING:

Beat together 2 cups confectioners' sugar, 1/4 cup mashed bananas, 2 tablespoons softened butter or margarine and 1/2 teaspoon vanilla. If necessary, beat in additional confectioners' sugar to make of spreading consistency.

🌱 PEANUT BUTTER COOKIES 🌱

A long time favorite of almost everyone.

- 1¼ cups all-purpose flour
- ¼ teaspoon soda
- ½ teaspoon baking powder
- ¼ teaspoon salt
- ½ cup butter, softened
- ½ cup peanut butter (I prefer the chunky type)
- ½ cup sugar
- ½ cup brown sugar
- 1 egg
- 1 teaspoon vanilla

Preheat oven to 375°F.

Do *not grease* cookie sheets. Combine flour, soda, baking powder and salt. Set aside. Cream butters until light, add both sugars and cream very thoroughly. Beat in egg, then stir in vanilla. Add flour-mixture in 2 or 3 portions, mixing until smooth after each. Chill dough for an hour or so. Measure level tablespoon of dough onto cookie sheets two inches apart. Press twice with tines of fork that has first been dipped in cold water, to make crisscross pattern on top. Bake 10 to 12 minutes or until delicately brown. Remove immediately from baking sheet to cake racks to cool.

BREAKFAST OR BRUNCH

Some of these recipes will be a change of pace for breakfast. Some are for special occasions.

🦌 BLUEBERRY PANCAKES 🦌

These are yummie, but offer no help with any kind of diet!

Serves 4.

- 1 egg
- 1 cup milk
- 2 tablespoons sour cream
- 1/3 cup sugar
- 1 cup flour
- 1/4 teaspoon salt
- 1/2 teaspoon mace*
- 1 tablespoon baking powder
- 2 tablespoons melted butter
- 1 cup blueberries, fresh or frozen (thawed and drained if frozen)

In a small bowl whisk together egg, milk, sour cream and sugar. In a larger bowl, sift together flour, salt, mace and baking powder. Stir in egg mixture and beat well with wire whisk. Add the melted butter and stir until mixed. Fold in blueberries. Cook on a lightly *greased* griddle.

*Mace is a spice made from the external covering of nutmeg. It has a different flavor than nutmeg and the two are not interchangeable.

🦃 BRUNCH ENCHILADAS 🦃

Makes 8 servings.

- 2 cups ground, fully cooked ham
- 1 1/2 cups shredded Cheddar cheese plus another cup of shredded Cheddar to sprinkle on top
- 1/2 cup sliced green onions
- 1 4-ounce can chopped chili peppers, drained
- 8 7-inch flour tortillas
- Cornmeal
- 4 beaten eggs
- 2 cups light cream or milk
- 1 tablespoon all-purpose flour
- 1/4 teaspoon garlic powder
- Few drops Tabasco sauce

Preheat oven to 350°F.

In a bowl combine ground ham, 1 1/2 cups cheese, onion and chili peppers. Place 1/3 cup of the mixture at one end of each tortilla; roll up. Arrange tortillas, seam side down, in a *greased* and *cornmeal-sprinkled* 12x8x2-inch baking dish. Combine eggs, cream, flour, garlic powder and Tabasco sauce. Pour over tortillas. Cover and refrigerate at least 4 hours or overnight. Bake, covered, for about 1 hour or until set. Sprinkle with 1 cup shredded cheese. Let stand 10 minutes.

❦ A TIP FOR SCRAMBLED EGGS ❦

Try using cold water instead of milk in the eggs.

The eggs will be fluffier and more tender.

❦ FRENCH TOAST ❦

You can use regular sliced bread, but egg bread, sliced thick, is better.

- 6 slices of day-old egg bread, sliced 1 inch thick
- 1 1/2 cups half and half
- 1 egg
- 1/4 teaspoon vanilla
- 2 tablespoons powdered sugar, divided
- Melted butter
- Maple syrup

Beat half and half, egg, vanilla and 1 tablespoon powdered sugar together and strain through a fine sieve into a large bowl. Soak bread briefly in egg mixture and place in a pan containing 1/2-inch melted butter. Cook slowly and turn often. Before serving, sprinkle with the remaining powdered sugar. Serve plain or with maple syrup.

🍎 APPLE FRITTERS 🍎

This recipe came from Stephenson's Apple Farm in Kansas City, Missouri. It is an extra special breakfast treat.

Serves 6.

- 2 cups flour
- 2 teaspoons baking powder
- 1 teaspoon salt
- 1 cup milk
- 2 eggs, separated
- 1 tablespoon sugar
- 2 cups peeled and sliced apples
- Oil for frying
- Maple syrup

Beat yolks and whites separately and set aside. Combine flour, baking powder and salt. Set aside. Heat milk until more than lukewarm. Add slowly to beaten egg yolks and sugar. Add flour and whites of eggs. Stir together. Then add slices of apples. Drop into hot oil in large spoonfuls and fry until light brown.

Serve with maple syrup.

🦌 CHRISTMAS BRUNCH CASSEROLE 🦌

Serves 10 to 12.

- 12 slices white bread with crusts trimmed off, buttered and cubed
- 1/2 pound Velveeta cheese, cubed
- 6 eggs, beaten
- 1 quart milk
- 1 teaspoon salt
- 8 slices bacon, fried crisp, drained and crumbled

Preheat oven to 325°F.

Using a 2½-quart casserole, put all of the bread in the bottom of the dish. Put cheese cubes over bread. Add milk and salt to beaten eggs, mix well and pour over cheese. Refrigerate at least twelve hours or overnight. Bake 1 to 1½ hours. Sprinkle bacon over casserole for the last ten minutes of baking time.

🐝 SAUSAGE AND CHEESE STRATA 🐝

This is a great breakfast or brunch dish. You can use bacon, fried crisp, instead of the sausage or make one side with sausage and one side with bacon.

Serves 8 to 10.

    1 pound breakfast sausages
    8 slices of bread, with crusts removed and cubed
    1 cup grated Cheddar cheese
    4 eggs
  2½ cups milk
    1 teaspoon salt
    1 teaspoon dry mustard
    1 can mushroom soup*
    1 small can mushrooms, drained
      Additional small amount of milk

Preheat oven to 350°F.

Cook sausages, drain, cut into pieces and set aside. Put bread into oblong (12x9) casserole dish. Cover bread with cheese and sausages. Beat together eggs, 2½ cups milk, salt and dry mustard. Pour over bread mixture, cover and refrigerate overnight. When ready to bake, mix mushroom soup, mushrooms and a little milk to make a smooth mixture. Pour over bread mixture. Bake for 1 hour or until puffed and golden.

*There are many versions of this recipe. You can delete the mushroom soup, mushrooms and additional milk and still have a great dish.

BEVERAGES

Liqueurs, Punches and Such

❦ CREME DE MENTHE ❦

  7½ cups water
  6½ cups super fine sugar*
    1 pint of 190-proof grain alcohol
    3 tablespoons pure peppermint extract
    1 tablespoon green food coloring

Boil sugar and water 10 minutes, covered. Cool completely. (This is very important.) Add alcohol and mix thoroughly. Add peppermint and food coloring. Mix well. Bottle and keep in your liquor cabinet. Your friends will not know it is homemade unless you tell them.

*You'll find this along with the other sugars in your grocery store.

❦ KAHLUA ❦

  3½ cups water
    3 cups sugar
  3½ tablespoons Maxim Freeze Dried coffee
  1½ tablespoons pure vanilla extract
   ½ pint pure grain alcohol

Put sugar in water and simmer until sugar dissolves, then add coffee and stir. Let cool completely. (This is very important.) Add 1½ tablespoons pure vanilla extract and ½ pint pure grain alcohol. Place in container and store in liquor cabinet.

❦ BAILEY'S IRISH CREAM ❦

    4 eggs
    1 can Eagle Brand sweetened condensed milk
    8 ounces whiskey
  1/4 teaspoon coconut extract
    2 teaspoons vanilla extract
    2 tablespoons Hershey's chocolate syrup

Beat eggs in blender. Add other ingredients and blend until smooth. Refrigerate.

❦ WINE SPRITZERS ❦

Serves 8 to 10.

    1 25-ounce bottle white wine
    1 28-ounce bottle club soda
       Lemon slices
       Lime slices

Combine wine and club soda; mix gently. Pour into ice-filled glasses; garnish with slices of fruit.

🦌 PITCHER BLOODY MARYS 🦌

Makes 1¾ quarts.

- 1 46-ounce can tomato juice
- 1 cup vodka
- 2 tablespoons Worcestershire sauce
- ½ teaspoon Tabasco hot sauce
- ¼ teaspoon pepper
- ⅛ teaspoon celery salt
- Juice of 2 lemons
- Celery sticks

Combine all ingredients except celery sticks; stir well. Serve over ice; garnish with celery sticks.

🦌 BANANA DAIQUIRIS 🦌

Makes 6 servings.

- 1 ripe medium banana
- 2 ounces (¼ cup) banana liqueur
- 1 ounce (2 tablespoons) dark rum
- 1 tablespoon sugar or to taste
- ½ teaspoon fresh lemon juice
- Crushed ice
- 6 maraschino cherries

Combine banana, banana liqueur, rum, sugar and lemon juice with scoop of crushed ice in blender container. Mix well, adding crushed ice until blender is filled. Pour into glasses and garnish with cherries.

Strawberry daiquiris can be made with the same recipe. Substitute 4 ounces (½ cup) partially thawed frozen strawberries in syrup for the banana, and strawberry liqueur for the banana liqueur.

DAIQUIRI SLUSH

16 servings.

- 3 6-ounce cans frozen lemonade
- 1 6-ounce can frozen limeade
- 8 cups water
- 1 fifth light rum or vodka

Mix all ingredients. Pour into plastic containers and freeze. Stir occasionally. Daiquiri is always "mushy frozen" and ready to serve topped with a cherry.

PARTY PUNCH

Makes about 20 cups.

- 1 quart orange juice, chilled
- 1 quart cranberry juice, chilled
- 2 33-ounce bottles ginger ale, chilled
- 2 33-ounce bottles champagne, chilled
- Fresh strawberries for garnish

Combine orange juice and cranberry juice in punch bowl. Gently stir in ginger ale and champagne. Garnish with strawberries.

❦ MARGARITAS FOR A CROWD ❦

Makes 16 servings.

- 1 lime wedge
- 1/2 cup coarse kosher salt
- 2 cups tequila
- 2 1/2 cups grapefruit juice, fresh or reconstituted
- 1 1/2 cups orange-flavored liqueur
- 1/2 cup fresh lime juice

Rub rims of 16 glasses with lime wedge. Dip into plate of coarse salt; set aside up to 6 hours.

In large pitcher combine tequila, grapefruit juice, liqueur and lime juice. (Can be made ahead to this point. Cover and refrigerate up to 24 hours.) Stir and pour into salt-rimmed glasses, over ice.

❦ CHAMPAGNE PUNCH ❦

Makes 15 servings.

- Ice ring
- 1 magnum (two-fifths of a gallon) of pink champagne
- 1 fifth Rose wine
- 1 pint vodka
- 1 28-ounce bottle soda

Place frozen ice ring in bottom of punch bowl and pour chilled liqueurs and soda over.

🍒 PINA COLADA PUNCH 🍒

Ice ring
1 20-ounce can crushed pineapple, undrained
2 15-ounce cans cream of coconut
1 46-ounce can pineapple juice, chilled
2 cups light rum
1 32-ounce bottle club soda, chilled

Prepare ice ring in advance. In blender container, combine crushed pineapple and cream of coconut; blend until smooth. In large punch bowl, combine pineapple mixture, pineapple juice and rum. Just before serving, add club soda and ice.

❦ OJ AND VODKA SLUSH ❦

Freezer-ready anytime!

Makes 25 servings.

- 1/2 cup sugar
- 2 cups water
- 1 12-ounce can frozen orange juice, thawed
- 1 12-ounce can frozen lemonade, thawed
- 1 quart water
- 3 cups vodka
- 1/2 cup lemon juice
- 3 16-ounce bottles lemon-lime carbonated beverage

In medium saucepan, boil sugar and 2 cups water for 3 minutes; cool completely. (This is very important.) In large non-metal container, combine sugar mixture orange juice, lemonade, 1 quart water, vodka and lemon juice. Cover and freeze.

Before serving, let thaw at room temperature 15 minutes to soften and blend, stirring occasionally. Spoon 1/2 cup into glass; add 1/4 cup lemon-lime beverage and stir. Garnish with orange slices and maraschino cherries.

INDEX

A

A Tip for Scrambled Eggs 291
A Very Special Spinach Salad 47
Aloha Crisps 18
Ambrosia 267
Appetizers 1
    Aloha Crisps 18
    Bacon Dip 4
    Barbecued Cocktail Sausages 6
    Braunschweiger Dip 6
    Chicken Pillows 14
    Chile Con Queso 24
    Chinese Fried Walnuts 29
    Clam Appetizers 16
    Clamdiggers Dip 4
    Cottage and Blue Cheese Dip 3
    Crabmeat Dip 5
    Cracker Spread 19
    Deviled Ham Spread 19
    Egg Rolls 8
    Egg Rolls with Shrimp 10
    Fried Shrimp Wonton 12
    Guacamole 7
    Herb Dip with Dill and Chives 3
    Hot Crabmeat Canapes 17
    Korean Chicken Wings 26
    Marinated Mushrooms 21
    Meow Mix 23
    Mushroom-Cheese Appetizers 28
    Party Sausage Biscuits 18
    Reuben Appetizers 22
    Sausage Triangles 27
    Scallion and Blue Cheese Dip 5
    Spicy Cream Cheese Dip 7
    Surprise Cheese Puffs 20
    Tex-Mex Dip 25

Apples

    Apple Fritters 292
    Apple Glazed Pork Roast 128
    Golden Apple Torte 260
    Roast Pork with Sweet Potatoes and Apples 129

Apple Fritters 292
Apple Glazed Pork Roast 128
Au Jus 94

ℬ

Bacon Dip 4
Bailey's Irish Cream 298
Baked Drumsticks 157
Baked Lasagna 112
Baked Oysters with Bread Crumbs and Garlic 187
Baked Vidalia Onions 199
Banana Daiquiris 299
Banana Drop Cookies 284
Banana Pudding 262
Banana Walnut Muffins 236
Banana-Nut Bread 242

Barbecue
    Barbecued Cocktail Sausages 6
    Barbecued Pot Roast 97
    Brazilian Barbecued Beef 100
    Chinese-Hawaiian Barbecued Ribs 134
    Special Steak B-B-Q 96
    Spicy Barbecued Short Ribs 98

Barbecued Cocktail Sausages 6
Barbecued Pot Roast 97
Basic French Dressing 35

Beef and Veal 87
    Baked Lasagna 112
    Barbecued Pot Roast 97
    Beef Burgundy 108
    Beef Peperonata 105
    Beef Stroganoff 103

Braised Veal Shanks 115
Brazilian Barbecued Beef 100
Broiled Beef Tenderloin 90
Burritos 111
Grilled Reuben Sandwiches 121
"Hot" Stir-Fried Beef 118
London Broil 104
Meat Ball Stroganoff 110
Meat Loaf 109
Minute Steaks in Parsley Butter 104
Paul's Roast Beef 95
Pepper Steak 117
Pot Roast with Vegetables 93
Roast Brisket 89
Roast Tenderloin 92
Rolled Stuffed Steak 102
Salisbury Bourguignonne 107
Special Steak B-B-Q 96
Spicy Barbecued Short Ribs 98
Standing Rib Roast 94
Stir-Fried Beef with String Beans 119
Swiss Steak 101
Veal Cordon Bleu 114
Beef Burgundy 108
Beef Peperonata 105
Beef Stroganoff 103
Beverages 295
Bailey's Irish Creme 298
Banana Daiquiris 299
Champagne Punch 301
Creme de Menthe 297
Daiquiri Slush 300
Kahlua 297
Margaritas for a Crowd 301
OJ and Vodka Slush 303
Party Punch 300
Pina Colada Punch 302
Pitcher Bloody Marys 299
Wine Spritzers 298

Biscuits
    Buttermilk Biscuits 232
    Southern Biscuits 232
Blackhawk Salad Bowl 60
Bloody Marys, Pitcher 299
Blue Cheese Salad Dressing 33
Blueberry Cobbler 255
Blueberry Lemon Pound Cake 256
Blueberry Muffins 239
Blueberry Pancakes 289
Bonnie's Potato Salad 49
Bourbon Balls 277
Braised Veal Shanks 115
Brandied Pork Steak 135
Brandied Tomato Gravy 91
Braunschweiger Dip 6
Brazilian Barbecued Beef 100
Breads, Muffins and Such 225
    Banana-Nut Bread 242
    Banana Walnut Muffins 236
    Blueberry Muffins 239
    Buttermilk Biscuits 232
    Chive and Black Pepper Corn Bread 227
    Corny Corn Bread 228
    Cranberry Bread 240
    Dilly Cheese Bread 233
    Garlic Bread 234
    Golden Corn Bread 230
    Hush Puppies 231
    Oat 'n Orange Muffins 237
    Parmesan Pastry Twists 235
    Pumpkin Bread 241
    Pumpkin Muffins 238
    Southern Corn Bread 229
    Southern Biscuits 232
Breakfast or Brunch 287
    A Tip for Scrambles Eggs 291
    Apple Fritters 292
    Blueberry Pancakes 289
    Brunch Enchiladas 290

Christmas Brunch Casserole 293
French Toast 291
Sausage and Cheese Strata 294
Broccoli Marinade 202
Broiled Beef Tenderloin 90
Broiled Chicken 166
Broiled Monkfish 185
Broiled Mustard Pork Chops 138
Bronzed Chicken Breast 160
Brook Trout Stuffed with Crabmeat 182
Brunch Enchiladas 290
Buffet Bean Salad 59
Burritos 111
Butterflied Loin of Pork 125
Buttermilk Biscuits 232

C

Caesar's Salad 36
Caramel Bananas with Rum 266
Caramel Brownies 282
Caraway Cabbage 200
Cauliflower Salad 46
Champagne Punch 301
Cheesy Broccoli Casserole 201
Cheesy Potato Bake 219
Chef's Salad Bowl 41
Cherry Surprise Balls 274
Chesapeake Crab Cakes 190
Chicken and Pasta in Cream Sauce 158
Chicken Breast - Eden Isle 168
Chicken Diane 159
Chicken Elegant 169
Chicken Frisco 166
Chicken Hekka 151
Chicken or Turkey with Rice Soup 85
Chicken Parmigiana 155
Chicken Pillows 14

Chicken Pot Roast 152
Chicken with Swiss Cheese and Prosciutto 154
Chile Con Queso 24
Chilled Zucchini Soup 82
Chinese Egg Drop Soup 78
Chinese Fried Walnuts 29
Chinese Pork Roast or Spareribs 132
Chinese-Hawaiian Barbecued Ribs 134
Chive and Black Pepper Corn Bread 227
Chocolate Luscious Pie 248
Chocolate Pie 253
Christmas Brunch Casserole 293
Clam Appetizers 16
Clam Chowder 79
Clamdiggers Dip 4
Coconut Cream Pie 246
Colonial Bread Pudding 264
Concorde Salad 39
Cookies and Bars 271
    Banana Drop Cookies 284
    Bourbon Balls 277
    Caramel Brownies 282
    Cherry Surprise Balls 274
    Date Filled Squares 279
    Oatmeal Cookies 280
    O'Henry Bars 275
    Orange Fruitcake Bars 278
    Peanut Blossoms 283
    Peanut Butter Cookies 286
    Pecanettes 276
    Pineapple Cookies 281
    Raisin Oatmeal Cookies 273
Corn Breads
    Chive and Black Pepper Corn Bread 227
    Corny Corn Bread 228
    Golden Corn Bread 230
    Hush Puppies 231
    Southern Corn Bread 229
Corny Corn Bread 228
Cottage and Blue Cheese Dip 3

Country Captain 150
Country-Style Chicken Kiev 167
Country-Style Spareribs and Potatoes in
 Basil Tomato Sauce 130
Crab-Filled Jumbo Mushrooms 188
Crabmeat Dip 5
Cracker Spread 19
Cranberry Bread 240
Cranberry Crisp 263
Cream of Broccoli Soup 81
Creamed Ham and Artichokes Casserole 144
Creamy Garlic Dressing 35
Creamy Pepper Dressing 34
Creme de Menthe 297
Cucumbers in Sour Cream 57

D

Daiquiri Slush 300
Date Filled Squares 279
Desserts 243
    Ambrosia 267
    Banana Pudding 262
    Blueberry Cobbler 255
    Blueberry Lemon Pound Cake 256
    Caramel Bananas with Rum 266
    Chocolate Luscious Pie 248
    Chocolate Pie 253
    Coconut Cream Pie 246
    Colonial Bread Pudding 264
    Cranberry Crisp 263
    Golden Apple Torte 260
    Grasshopper Pie 245
    Kahlua Parfait 270
    Lemon Meringue Pie 250
    Martha's Rice Pudding 261
    Mile-High Raspberry Pie 252
    Old-Time Fried Pies 268

Pecan Pie 254
Raspberry Walnut Torte 258
Rebecca Sauce 265
Deviled Ham Spread 19
Dilled Green Bean Salad 55
Dilly Cheese Bread 233
Dressings, *see* Salad Dressings

E

Egg Rolls 8
Egg Rolls with Shrimp 10
Eggs
A Tip for Scrambled Eggs 291
Christmas Brunch Casserole 293
Chinese Egg Drop Soup 78
Egg Rolls 8
Egg Rolls with Shrimp 10
Sausage and Cheese Strata 294
Shrimp Egg Foo Yong 177

F

Fillets of Sole in Creole Sauce 193
Fish, *see* Seafood
Fish and Chip Bake 192
Flounder with Shrimp Sauce 184
French Onion Soup 86
French Potato Salad 50
French Toast 291
French-Fried Mushrooms 211
Fried Eggplant 206
Fried Shrimp Wonton 12

G

Garlic Bread 234
German-Style Pork Schnitzel 126
Glazed Carrots 203
Golden Apple Torte 260
Golden Corn Bread 230
Golden Crunch Fried Chicken 148
Golden Pan-Fried Mushrooms 211
Grasshopper Pie 245
Greek Salad 38
Green Bean Bake 212
Grilled Reuben Sandwiches 121
Grilled Salmon with Mustard Dill Sauce 186
Guacamole 7

H

Ham, *see* Pork
Ham and Cheese Sandwiches 141
Ham Fried Rice 142
Hash Brown Cheese Bake 220
Herb Dip with Dill and Chives 3
Herb Grilled Chicken 149
Hot Chicken Supreme 164
Hot Crabmeat Canapes 17
Hot Mustard Sauce 12
Hot 'n Saucy Turkey Sandwiches 162
"Hot" Stir-Fried Beef 118
Hungarian Pork Paprika 137
Hush Puppies 231

K

Kahlua 297
Kahlua Parfait 270
Korean Chicken Wings 26

L

Lasagna, Baked 112
Lazy Day Oven Stew 70
Lemon Meringue Pie 250
Lentil Soup with Ham 75
Light Tomato-Vegetable Soup 84
London Broil 104
Louisiana Style Baked Shrimp 173

M

Macaroni and Cheese Deluxe 215
Margaritas for a Crowd 301
Marinated Mushrooms 21
Marinated String Beans 56
Marnie's Great Potatoes 221
Martha's Rice Pudding 261
Meat Ball Stroganoff 110
Meat Loaf 109
Meow Mix 23
Mile-High Raspberry Pie 252
Minorcan Clam Chowder 80
Minute Steaks in Parsley Butter 104
Muffins, *see* Breads, Muffins and Such
Mushroom Stuffing 90
Mushroom-Cheese Appetizers 28

N

New Potato Salad with Herbs and Shallots 52
New Potatoes and Peas 223
No Peek Chicken 165

O

Oat 'n Orange Muffins 237
Oatmeal Cookies 280
O'Henry Bars 275
OJ and Vodka Slush 303
Old-Time Fried Pies 268
Old-Time Pork Turnovers 140
Orange Fruitcake Bars 278
Orient Express Chicken Salad 43

P

Pan-Roasted Potatoes 223
Parmesan Chicken Breast 153
Parmesan Pastry Twists 235
Party Punch 300
Party Sausage Biscuits 18
Paul's Roast Beef 95
Peanut Blossoms 283
Peanut Butter Cookies 286
Pecan Pie 254
Pecanettes 276
Pepper Steak 117
Pies
    Chocolate Luscious Pie 248
    Chocolate Pie 253
    Coconut Cream Pie 246
    Grasshopper Pie 245
    Lemon Meringue Pie 250
    Mile-High Raspberry Pie 252
    Old-Time Fried Pies 268
    Pecan Pie 254
Pina Colada Punch 302
Pineapple Cookies 281
Pineapple Shrimp 178
Pitcher Bloody Marys 299
Plaza III Steak Soup 72
Poor Man's Crab Casserole 191

Pork 123
        Apple Glazed Pork Roast 128
        Brandied Pork Steak 135
        Broiled Mustard Pork Chops 138
        Butterflied Loin of Pork 125
        Chinese-Hawaiian Barbecued Ribs 134
        Chinese Pork Roast or Spareribs 132
        Country-Style Spareribs and Potatoes in
            Basil Tomato Sauce 130
        Creamed Ham and Artichokes Casserole 144
        German-Style Pork Schnitzel 126
        Ham and Cheese Sandwiches 141
        Ham Fried Rice 142
        Hungarian Pork Paprika 137
        Old-Time Pork Turnovers 140
        Pork Steaks, Chinese Style 136
        Roast Pork with Sweet Potatoes and Apples 129
        Sizzlin' Pork Chops 139
        Sliced Ham with Asparagus Spears and Egg Sauce 143
Pork Steaks, Chinese Style 136
Portuguese Chicken 156
Portuguese Vegetable Soup 71
Pot Roast with Vegetables 93
Potato Pancakes 222
Potato Salads
        Bonnie's Potato Salad 49
        French Potato Salad 50
        New Potato Salad with Herbs and Shallots 52
Potatoes, *see* Side Dishes
Poultry 145
        Baked Drumsticks 157
        Broiled Chicken 166
        Bronzed Chicken Breast 160
        Chicken and Pasta in Cream Sauce 158
        Chicken Breast - Eden Isle 168
        Chicken Diane 159
        Chicken Elegant 169
        Chicken Frisco 166
        Chicken Hekka 151
        Chicken Parmigiana 155

Chicken Pot Roast 152
Chicken with Swiss Cheese and Prosciutto 154
Country Captain 150
Country-Style Chicken Kiev 167
Golden Crunch Fried Chicken 148
Herb Grilled Chicken 149
Hot Chicken Supreme 164
Hot 'n Saucy Turkey Sandwiches 162
No Peek Chicken 165
Parmesan Chicken Breast 153
Portuguese Chicken 156
Southern Fried Chicken 147
Swiss Turkey Ham Bake 163
Turkey Mornay 161
Pumpkin Bread 241
Pumpkin Muffins 238

R

Raisin Oatmeal Cookies 273
Raspberry Walnut Torte 258
Ratatioule 205
Rebecca Sauce 265
Red Bean Soup 74
Red Cabbage Coleslaw 48
Red Wine Vinegar Dressing 45
Reuben Appetizers 22
Rice Pilaf 216
Roast Brisket 89
Roast Pork with Sweet Potatoes and Apples 129
Roast Tenderloin 92
Rolled Stuffed Steak 102
Rosoff's Coleslaw 58
Rouladen 102

S

Salad Dressings 31
    Basic French Dressing 35
    Blue Cheese Salad Dressing 33
    Creamy Garlic Dressing 35
    Creamy Pepper Dressing 34
    Red Wine Vinegar Dressing 45
    Vinaigrette Dressing 34

Salads 31
    A Very Special Spinach Salad 47
    Blackhawk Salad Bowl 60
    Bonnie's Potato Salad 49
    Buffet Bean Salad 59
    Caesar's Salad 36
    Cauliflower Salad 46
    Chef's Salad Bowl 41
    Concorde Salad 39
    Cucumbers in Sour Cream 57
    Dilled Green Bean Salad 55
    French Potato Salad 50
    Greek Salad 38
    Marinated String Beans 56
    New Potato Salad with Herbs and Shallots 52
    Orient Express Chicken Salad 43
    Red Cabbage Coleslaw 48
    Rosoff's Coleslaw 58
    Spaghetti Salad 54
    Strawberry Nut Salad 62
    Strawberry Souffle Salads 63
    Summer's Best Green Salad 42
    Tomato and Chick Pea Salad 44
    Tossed Salads 40
    Waldorf Salad 64

Salisbury Bourguignonne 107
Salmon Fritters 194

Sandwiches
    Grilled Reuben Sandwiches 121
    Ham and Cheese Sandwiches 141
    Hot 'n Saucy Turkey Sandwiches 162
    Tuna Bunsteads 195

Sausage and Cheese Strata 294
Sausage Ragout 67
Sausage Triangles 27
Sauteed Shredded Zucchini 209
Sauteed Zucchini with Carrots 207
Scallion and Blue Cheese Dip 5
Seafood 171
    Baked Oysters with Bread Crumbs and Garlic 187
    Broiled Monkfish 185
    Brook Trout Stuffed with Crabmeat 182
    Chesapeake Crab Cakes 190
    Crab-Filled Jumbo Mushrooms 188
    Fillets of Sole in Creole Sauce 193
    Fish and Chip Bake 192
    Flounder with Shrimp Sauce 184
    Grilled Salmon with Mustard Dill Sauce 186
    Louisiana Style Baked Shrimp 173
    Pineapple Shrimp 178
    Poor Man's Crab Casserole 191
    Salmon Fritters 194
    Shrimp Casserole 174
    Shrimp Creole 175
    Shrimp Egg Foo Yong 177
    Superb Seafood Casserole 181
    Tempura Shrimp 180
    Tuna Bunsteads 195
    Velvet Shrimp 176
Shrimp Casserole 174
Shrimp Creole 175
Shrimp Egg Foo Yong 177
Side Dishes 197
    Baked Vidalia Onions 199
    Broccoli Marinade 202
    Caraway Cabbage 200
    Cheesy Broccoli Casserole 201
    Cheesy Potato Bake 219
    French-Fried Mushrooms 211
    Fried Eggplant 206
    Glazed Carrots 203
    Golden Pan-Fried Mushrooms 211

Green Bean Bake 212
Hash Brown Cheese Bake 220
Macaroni and Cheese Deluxe 215
Marnie's Great Potatoes 221
New Potatoes and Peas 223
Pan-Roasted Potatoes 223
Potato Pancakes 222
Ratatioule 205
Rice Pilaf 216
Sauteed Shredded Zucchini 209
Sauteed Zucchini with Carrots 207
Spanish Rice 217
Steamed Vegetables 199
Stir-Fried Snow Peas 213
Stuffed Potatoes 224
Superb Vegetable Casserole 214
Sweet and Sour Beets 204
Turmeric Rice Pilaf 218
Zucchini Parmesan 208
Zucchini Sticks 210
Sizzlin' Pork Chops 139
Soups and Stews 65
    Chicken or Turkey with Rice Soup 85
    Chilled Zucchini Soup 82
    Chinese Egg Drop Soup 78
    Clam Chowder 79
    Cream of Broccoli Soup 81
    French Onion Soup 86
    Lentil Soup with Ham 75
    Lazy Day Oven Stew 70
    Light Tomato-Vegetable Soup 84
    Minorcan Clam Chowder 80
    Plaza III Steak Soup 72
    Portuguese Vegetable Soup 71
    Red Bean Soup 74
    Sausage Ragout 67
    Southwest Beef Stew 68
    Vegetable Beef Soup 73
    Wonton Soup 76
Southern Biscuits 232

Southern Corn Bread 229
Southern Fried Chicken 147
Southwest Beef Stew 68
Spaghetti Salad 54
Spanish Rice 217
Spareribs, *see* Pork Section
Special Steak B-B-Q 96
Spicy Barbecued Short Ribs 98
Spicy Cream Cheese Dip 7
Standing Rib Roast 94
Steamed Vegetables 199
Stews, *see* Soups and Stews
Stir-Fried Beef with String Beans 119
Stir-Fried Snow Peas 213
Strawberry Nut Salad 62
Strawberry Souffle Salads 63
Stuffed Potatoes 224
Summer's Best Green Salad 42
Superb Seafood Casserole 181
Superb Vegetable Casserole 214
Surprise Cheese Puffs 20
Sweet and Sour Beets 204
Sweet and Sour Sauce 13
Swiss Steak 101
Swiss Turkey Ham Bake 163

T

Tempura Shrimp 180
Tex-Mex Dip 25
Tomato and Chick Pea Salad 44
Tossed Salads 40
Tumeric Rice Pilaf 218
Tuna Bunsteads 195
Turkey Mornay 161

V

Veal, *see* Beef and Veal
Veal Cordon Bleu 114
Vegetables, *see* Side Dishes
Vegetable Beef Soup 73
Velvet Shrimp 176
Vinaigrette Dressing 34

W

Waldorf Salad 64
Wine Spritzers 298
Wonton Soup 76

Z

Zucchini Parmesan 208
Zucchini Sticks 210